The Psychology Student's Survival Guide

Robert S. Feldman

University of Massachusetts at Amherst

Sara Pollak Levine

Hampshire College

McGraw-Hill College

Boston   Burr Ridge, IL   Dubuque, IA   Madison, WI   New York   San Francisco   St. Louis
Bangkok   Bogotá   Caracas   Lisbon   London   Madrid
Mexico City   Milan   New Delhi   Seoul   Singapore   Sydney   Taipei   Toronto

McGraw-Hill College

A Division of The McGraw-Hill Companies

2 3 4 5 6 7 8 9 0 QPD/QPD 9 0 9

ISBN 0-07-232521-6

www.mhhe.com

Table of Contents

Preface

The Psychology Student's Survival Guide is designed to help students achieve success in psychology. Using a few central organizing principles, embodied in the abbreviation *P.O.W.E.R.* (Prepare, Organize, Work, Evaluate, and Rethink), **The Psychology Student's Survival Guide** discusses the steps necessary to flourish as a student of psychology. Through active reading of this book and completion of the numerous exercises in each chapter, psychology students can learn ways to increase their mastery of psychology and other academic domains as well.

The book is designed to accomplish three major goals:

- First and foremost, the book is meant to provide a systematic, balanced presentation of the skills required to achieve student success within the *P.O.W.E.R.* framework. Relying on strategies that have been proven by research to be effective, the book provides specific techniques for achieving success as a psychology student. It includes a variety of activities, presenting diagnostic questionnaires, diaries, observational exercises, case study analysis, and other procedures that provide practical advice leading to an increase in academic expertise.

- The second goal of the book is to make readers critically thinking consumers of information. Critical thinking skills are crucial to success, and dealing effectively with the array of information that the world presents—via the media, the world wide web, and even other's viewpoints—is essential. As communication networks expand and evolve, success in academic and other domains will increasingly revolve around the ability to sort through and evaluate information. Consequently, a primary goal of **The Psychology Student's Survival Guide** is to develop readers' critical thinking skills.

- Finally, the third goal of the book is one that underlies the first three: making the book engaging, accessible, and interesting to students—in short, user-friendly. Learning psychology should be an enjoyable and fulfilling experience, and this book seeks to give readers a sense of mastery and success. It is designed to engage and nurture students' intellectual curiosity.

To accomplish these goals, **The Psychology Student's Survival Guide** addresses topics of central importance to attaining success in psychology classes, including increasing reading and listening skills, improving public speaking abilities, and improving recall. It also covers making the most efficient use of time, using sources such as the World Wide Web to gather and manage information, and mastering the arts of note-taking, studying, and test-taking. Proven methods to increase proficiency in each of these areas are presented throughout the text, and numerous opportunities for practicing these new skills are presented within a number of different formats.

The Psychology Student's Survival Guide also includes several special features in each chapter. Among them are the following:

- **Prologues.** Each chapter begins with an example of psychology students who are encountering challenges in their studies. These students are confronting many of the same challenges every student faces in college.

- **In My Own Words.** These sections allow you to detail your academic experiences, successes and failures regarding each of the major topics contained in this book. Serving as a "jumping off point" for each of the topics, these sections encourage you to think deeply about each topic and identify your own particular strengths and weaknesses.

- **Try It!** Numerous questionnaires and exercises ask you to think about your present work habits, encourage you to explore new approaches to your coursework in psychology, and allow you to evaluate your understanding of the techniques presented in the text.

- **WEB P.O.W.E.R.** Found at the end of each chapter, these sections provide sites on the World Wide Web that supplement and expand upon information presented in each chapter.

By studying the material and completing the activities presented in **The Psychology Student's Survival Guide**, you will obtain the skills necessary to succeed in psychology classes. At the same time, you will better appreciate what the discipline of psychology has to offer and how it can enhance your understanding of the themselves and the world around them.

Chapter 1

You've Got P.O.W.E.R.:
Considering the Foundations of Student Success in Psychology

When Marsha Greene was 10, she went through some hard
times...her parents divorced, her brother went to live with her father, and
her grandfather died, all within the course of one year. Her only decent
memories of the following six months revolved around the time she
spent each week with Dr. Howard, her psychologist. At that time it
seemed as though her whole world was collapsing, but Dr. Howard was
always there to give her support.

These days, Marsha considers herself pretty "well-adjusted".
She just graduated high school, she's got great friends, and she's close
with both of her parents and her brother. Lately she's been thinking a lot
about what she wants to major in when she gets to college. She thought
about English or History because she loves to read, but she's pretty sure
it's going to be Psychology. She still has really positive memories of her
time with Dr. Howard and she'd like to be able to help other kids deal
with their problems. So all she has to do now is get through the
coursework and get a degree. High school wasn't too bad, but can she
really handle college-level work? Does she really belong in college?

Looking Ahead

As you read this, thousands of Marsha Greenes are asking themselves the same questions, and
working to fulfill their own dreams. Maybe you're a recent high school graduate who's always been
intrigued by psychology, and for you earning a degree in psychology has always seemed to be just a step
on the natural path of your life. Or perhaps you are someone who has always yearned to earn a degree in
psychology but was forced by the surprises of life to defer it for many years. What kind of student will
you be? Perhaps academic pursuits are a real struggle for you. Perhaps they're relatively easy.

Whatever your background, studying psychology is a challenge. All of us have doubts of one sort
or another about our abilities. That's where this book comes in. It's designed to provide you with a
strategy that will bring you success—P.O.W.E.R. Learning. Based on proven principles developed over
the course of decades by psychologists and educators, P.O.W.E.R. Learning can help you learn the skills
that will ensure your success in the 21st century.

You'll find in P.O.W.E.R. Learning a variety of practical strategies, tactics, techniques, hints, and
tips. You'll keep a journal ("In My Own Words") and be able to trace the changes in your life over the
course of the term. You'll evaluate yourself on a variety of dimensions ("Try It!" questionnaires and
exercises) to help you figure out just who you are and what your strengths and weaknesses are. And in
the chapter prologues, you'll find the stories of college students, some similar to you and some very
different, who have dealt with the challenges of psychology in various ways.

This book is designed to be useful. It presents a great amount of information in a hands-on
format and in relatively short chunks. And it's meant to be used. It's probably the only book you'll use
in your college career that's supposed to be defaced. Write on the pages, underline words and sentences,
use a highlighter, circle key points, jot down notes, complete the questionnaires and journals right in the
book. The more you carry out the exercises, the more you'll get from the book.

In short, P.O.W.E.R. Learning is designed to help you achieve success in psychology. In this
first chapter, we'll lay out the background for the P.O.W.E.R. Learning system and learn its basics.

In My Own Words
My School Experiences

Note: Throughout this book, you will be given opportunities to write down your thoughts. These opportunities—called "In My Own Words"—can be thought of as journal entries in which you record your reactions to what you have read, your ideas, notes, questions, and concerns. You may want to agree or disagree, but above all, be honest. If you return to these entries later, you may be surprised at the changes they record.

What are some successful experiences you have had in school? Think back as far as you can.

Why were they successful? What are their common elements? Think of the teacher's methods, the subjects you were studying, how you did your work, interactions you had with others, and other elements of these experiences.

What did you learn from them?

Were they always enjoyable? Did you ever learn something from experiences you disliked?

Did you ever have a "light bulb" experience—in which you suddenly "saw the light" about something that had seemed beyond understanding before? How did it happen?

What unsuccessful experiences or failures have you had in school?

Why?

What did these experiences have in common?

What did you learn from them?

Other comments:

What Is P.O.W.E.R. Learning?

P.O.W.E.R. Learning is a system designed to help you achieve your goals. It is a strategy that will bring you closer to accomplishing what you wish to—and sometimes have to—accomplish.

By breaking down tasks into a series of steps, P.O.W.E.R. Learning provides a systematic framework that increases the probability of your success. It works for both academic and nonacademic tasks, ranging from writing a college paper to purchasing the weekly groceries.

But always keep this fact in mind: *You* are the only one who can make P.O.W.E.R. Learning succeed. Without your personal investment in the process, it will be a hollow shell, words on paper. You will have to supply effort and practice to make it work for you.

Relax, though: You already know P.O.W.E.R. Learning. You've already been accepted into college and learned to read. You've also probably held down a job, had a first date, mowed the lawn, picked up the groceries, taken a vacation. Each of these accomplishments—and don't underrate them, they are accomplishments—required that you use the elements of the P.O.W.E.R. Learning system. What we'll be doing throughout this book is simply making these elements explicit and clear, allowing you to harness the power of the system.

In this chapter we'll outline the basics of P.O.W.E.R. Learning, providing a general overview and spelling out the system's foundations and advantages. In each future chapter, we'll apply the system to the specific area addressed in that chapter. But it's important for you to understand the fundamentals of P.O.W.E.R. Learning, so let's get started. A guarantee to make it worthwhile: If you master P.O.W.E.R. Learning and use the system, you'll find yourself succeeding in your study of psychology and your everyday personal dealings.

Prepare

Chinese philosopher Lao Tzu said that travelers taking a long journey must begin with a single step.

He was dead wrong. Even before they take their first step, travelers need to know several things: what their destination is, how they're going to get there, how they'll know when they reach the destination, and what they'll do if they have trouble along the way.

Suppose, for instance, you wanted to visit your cousin's new apartment. Think about what you'd need to know even before you took the first step out of your own home:

- What's the address of the apartment?
- What are my options for getting there? Should I take a car, bus, subway? Should I hitchhike?
- Given the way I choose to take the trip, what will I need? Gas for the car? Bus fare? Subway tokens?
- What are some landmarks along the way so I know I'm headed in the right direction? How big is the apartment building? What color is it? Is it near anything I'll recognize?
- If I get lost, what should I do? Do I have the phone number at my destination to ask for help?
- How will I be sure I've arrived at the right place when I get there?

Goal-setting strategies. Before we seek to accomplish any task, all of us do some form of planning. The trouble is that most of the time such planning is done without conscious thinking, as if we are on autopilot.

The key to success is to make sure that planning is systematic. The best way to plan systematically is to use *goal-setting* strategies. In many cases, goals are clear and direct. It's clear that our goal in washing dishes is to have the dishes end up clean and dry. We know that our goal at the gas station is to fill the car's tank with gas. We go to the post office to buy stamps and mail letters.

Other goals are not so clear-cut. In fact, often the more important the task, the less obvious are our goals. Let's take enrolling in psychology classes, for example. You probably had many goals in mind when you signed up for your psychology classes. List as many of the goals you have for taking psychology classes as you can think of.

Try It! #1
Goals for Enrolling in Psychology Classes

_____

_____

_____

_____

_____

_____

_____

_____

_____

_____

The goals you've listed most likely range from the specific ("getting a degree") to the more general and vague ("helping people"). What's the best way to set appropriate goals? Here are some guidelines:

- **Set both long-term and short-term goals.** **Long-term goals** are aims relating to major accomplishments that take some time to achieve. **Short-term goals** are relatively limited steps you would take on the road to accomplishing your long-term goals. For example, one of the primary reasons you're taking psychology classes is to achieve the long-term goal of getting a degree. But in order to reach that goal, you have to accomplish a series of short-term goals, such as completing a set of required courses, taking a series of elective courses, and choosing a major. Furthermore, even these short-term goals can be broken down into shorter-term goals. In order to complete a required course, for instance, you have to accomplish short-term goals, such as completing a paper, taking several tests, and so on.

- **Recognize your underlying values.** Goal-setting starts by knowing yourself. Start by assessing your **values**—the beliefs that you hold most strongly. Use this information, as well as assessing your strengths and weaknesses, to set short-term goals (which can be achieved in, say, a few weeks) and long-term goals (which take longer to accomplish).

- **Make goals realistic.** We'd all like to win gold medals at the Olympics or star in rock videos or write best-selling novels. Few of us are likely to achieve such goals. When we don't, we may make the mistake of reasoning that we are inept and lack ability. However, the problem has less to do with our abilities and more to do with poor goal-setting strategies. If goals are realistic, we are more likely to fulfill them.

- **State goals in terms of behavior that can be measured against current accomplishments.** Goals should represent some *measurable* change from a current set of circumstances. We want our behavior to change in some way that can usually be expressed in terms of numbers—to show an increase ("raise my grade point average 10 percent") or a decrease ("reduce wasted time by 2 hours each week"); to be maintained ("keep in touch with my friends by writing 4 letters each month"), developed ("participate in one workshop on critical thinking"), or restricted ("reduce my phone expenses 10 percent by speaking less on the telephone").

- **Goals should involve behavior over which you have control.** We all want world peace and an end to poverty. Few of us have the resources or capabilities to bring either about. On the other hand, it is realistic—and laudatory!—to want to work in small ways to help others, such as by becoming a Big Brother or Big Sister or volunteering at a local food bank.

- **Take ownership of your goals.** Make sure that the goals you choose are *your* goals, and not the goals of your parents, teachers, brothers and sisters, or friends. Trying to accomplish goals that "belong" to others is a recipe for disaster. If you're attending college only because others have told you to, and you have no commitment of your own, you'll find it hard to maintain the required enthusiasm—not to mention hard work—to succeed.

- **Identify how your short-term goals fit with your long-term goals.** Your goals should not be independent of one another. Instead, they should fit together into a larger dream of who you want to be. Every once in a while step back and consider how what you're doing today relates to the kind of person that you would ultimately like to be.

Given these goal-setting guidelines, let's revisit the goals that you listed earlier relating to your decision to take psychology classes. Rewrite each of those goals in terms that are realistic, measurable, and under your control.

Try It! #2
Goals for Enrolling in Psychology Classes (Revised)

_____
_____
_____
_____
_____
_____
_____
_____
_____
_____

Organize

By determining where you want to go and expressing your goals in terms that can be measured, you have already made a lot of progress. Your clear destination will make clearer the various options you have for reaching it, and will also help you know when you've arrived. You might think you're now ready to head out and begin the intellectual trip to student success. But no—there's still another step you must take before you get going. You now need to organize the resources you'll need in order to reach your goal.

The second step in P.O.W.E.R. Learning is to *organize* the tools you'll need to accomplish your goals. Building upon the goal-setting work you've undertaken in the *preparation* stage, you now need to determine the best way to accomplish the goals you've identified.

Your success in psychology will hinge to a large degree on the thoroughness of your organization for each task that faces you. In fact, one of the biggest mistakes that students make in college is plunging into an academic project—studying for a test, writing a paper, completing an in-class assignment—without being well organized.

Several kinds of organization are essential. On a basic level is organization involving the *physical aspects* of task completion. For instance, you need to ask yourself if you have the appropriate tools, such as pens, paper, and a calculator. If you're using a computer, do you have access to a printer? Is the printer working? Do you have an extra ink cartridge in case it runs out? Do you have the books and other materials you'll need to complete the assignment? Will the campus bookstore be open if you need anything else? Will the library be open when you need it? (Consider your frustration level if you plan to study the next day and you set out for the library to read the one book that you absolutely need—only to find the library closed.)

Intellectual organization is even more critical. Keeping your goals in mind, you'll need to organize the vast array of mental skills and the knowledge that you already have. How do you accomplish intellectual organization? By considering and reviewing the academic skills that you'll need to successfully complete the task at hand.

For example, if you're working on a statistics assignment, you'll want to consider the basic math skills that you'll need and brush up on them. Just bringing them into your active thinking will help you. Recalling and reviewing fundamental math skills, such as how to figure percentages and use decimals, will organize your thinking when you begin a new assignment. Similarly, you'd want to mentally review your understanding of Piaget's stages before beginning an assignment on cognitive development in children.

Why does creating an intellectual organization matter? The answer is that it provides a context when you actually begin to work. Educational researchers have found that "advance organizers," broad, general ideas related to new material, pave the way for better subsequent learning of the new material. The better your intellectual (as well as physical) organization for a task, the more successful you'll be.

Work

You're ready. The preliminaries are out of the way. You've *prepared* and you've *organized*. Now it's time to start actually doing the work.

In some ways this is the easy part, because—if you conscientiously carried out the preparation and organization stage—you should know exactly where you're headed and what you need to do to get there.

But it's not quite so easy, of course. How effectively you'll get down to the business at hand depends on a host of factors. Some are out of your control. There may be a power outage that closes down the library or a massive traffic jam that prevents you from getting to the campus. But other factors are—or should be—under your control. Instead of getting down to work, you may find yourself thinking up "useful" things to do—like finally hanging that picture that's been leaning against the wall for three months—or simply sitting as if captive in front of the TV. This kind of obstacle to work relates to motivation.

Motivation. "If I only had more motivation, I'd do so much better with my schoolwork." Or following my diet, or getting organized, or_____ (you fill in the blank).

All of us have said something like this at one time or another. We use the concept of **motivation**—or its lack—to explain why we just don't work hard at a task. But when we do that, we're fooling ourselves. We all have *some* motivation, that inner power and psychological energy that directs and fuels our behavior and allows us to persist, even when the going gets rough. Without any motivation, we'd never get out of bed in the morning and accomplish anything.

All of us are motivated. The key to success in and out of the classroom is to harness and direct that motivation. Thought of in this way, motivating ourselves becomes a little less intimidating. If we assume that we already have all the motivation we need, P.O.W.E.R. Learning becomes a matter of turning the skills we already possess into a habit. It becomes a matter of redirecting our psychological energies toward the *work* we wish to accomplish. But there's a key concept that underlies the control of motivation: viewing success as a result of effort.

Seeing effort as the cause of success. You've performed unusually well on a midterm exam. In fact, your instructor has complimented you on your performance. You think to yourself, "What great luck!" and "Pretty easy test."

This kind of thinking is known as making an **external attribution**. People who make external attributions assume that events are caused by factors outside of themselves, over which they have little

6

control. People making external attributions assume that it really doesn't matter how hard they work, because most events in their lives are caused by factors outside of themselves, which they can't control.

But notice the danger here. When you make an external attribution, you're sending yourself a message that hard work doesn't matter, that you're the pawn of circumstances. If you truly believed that, there'd be no reason to work hard at anything, because what happened to you would just reflect external factors that you didn't influence.

Suppose, though, that when you experienced success on a midterm exam you said to yourself, "Good job—I really studied hard on the exam." In this case, you're making an **internal attribution**. When we make internal attributions, we see the causes of events as due to our own behavior. We are in control of events: We perceive ourselves as the primary determinant of what happens to us. If we work harder or more efficiently, we assume we'll probably do better; if we slack off, we assume we'll do worse.

Few of us view the world purely in terms of either internal attributions or external attributions, but we all tend to take a characteristic approach to explaining what happens to us. Where do you stand? Check off if you agree or disagree with each of the following statements.

Try It! #3
Are Your Attributions External or Internal?

1. If a teacher is boring, I probably won't get a good grade in his or her class. ____ Agree ____ Disagree
2. When I do well on a test, it's usually because I've studied hard. ____ Agree ____ Disagree
3. I need help in getting myself to study effectively. ____ Agree ____ Disagree
4. Last-minute changes in plan don't bother me much. ____ Agree ____ Disagree
5. If I make a mistake, it's usually someone else's fault. ____ Agree ____ Disagree
6. Most of the time I am able to control what happens to me. ____ Agree ____ Disagree
7. When I get bad grades on a test, it's usually because the test is difficult. ____ Agree ____ Disagree
8. There's a strong relationship between how much time I put into an assignment and the grade I get on it. ____ Agree ____ Disagree
9. I find it hard to get up in the morning without someone to remind me. ____ Agree ____ Disagree
10. I see myself as self-motivated. ____ Agree ____ Disagree

If you agreed with most of the odd-numbered statements and disagreed with most of the even-numbered statements, you tend to make external attributions. On the other hand, if you agreed with most of the even-numbered statements and disagreed with most of the odd-numbered ones, you tend to view the world more in terms of internal attributions.

The kind of attributions people make is not unrelated to their success. For instance, students who normally make internal attributions usually do better in college. It's not hard to see why: When they are working on an assignment, they feel that the greater the effort they put forth, the greater their chances of success. So they work harder. They are positive thinkers, believing that they have control over their success. If they fail, they believe they can do better in the future. Failure just makes them try harder in the future.

In comparison, students who make external attributions are often less successful. They think that teachers give grades in subjective, biased ways. They see success as due to luck. They believe that the amount of work they put into an assignment doesn't really matter, because the outcome will be the result of chance factors. If they succeed it's because they have good luck or because the teacher felt like giving them a good grade. If they fail, they've been unlucky or the teacher was an unfair grader.

People aren't born making internal or external attributions. Instead, they develop an attributional style over time. If you tend to make external attributions, it is quite possible to change and to begin to view the world in terms of making more internal attributions. Here are some steps to take:

- **Take responsibility for your failures—and successes.** When you do poorly on a test, don't blame the teacher, the textbook, or a job that kept you from studying. Analyze the situation and see how you could have changed what you did to be more successful in the future. At the same time, when you're successful, think of the things you did to make the success occur.
- **Think positively.** Assume that the strengths that you have will allow you to succeed. The more effectively you work, the greater the success you'll experience.
- **Accept that you can't control everything.** Sometimes things are out of your control. Seek to understand which things can be changed and which cannot.

The key to excusing yourself properly is to be truthful to yourself and others, and to avoid placing blame on other people or on some force like fate. If circumstances that were truly out of your control—a broken computer, a power outage—prevented you from doing a task that you were supposed to do, allow yourself to accept the excuse, but do what you can to make up for it as quickly as possible and to avoid a similar situation in the future.

Evaluate

Great, I'm finished. I've done the work. It's time to hand in the worksheet, or take the test, or give the oral report.

It's natural to feel relief when you've finished the work necessary to fulfill the basic requirements of an assignment. After all, if you've written the five double-spaced pages required for an assignment, why shouldn't you heave a sigh of relief and just hand your paper in to the instructor?

The answer is that if you stop at this point, you'll almost be guaranteed a mediocre grade. Even the greatest work does not spring forth as the embodiment of perfection, meeting all the goals of its producer. In fact, the ultimate success of an activity is based on how closely it matches what it was intended to be. **Evaluation**, then—the assessment of the match between a product or activity and the goals it was intended to meet—is an essential step on the road to success.

Let's consider some steps that it makes sense to follow in evaluating what you've accomplished:

- **Take a moment to congratulate yourself.** Whether it's been studying for a test, writing a paper, preparing a review sheet, or reading an assignment, you've done something important. You've moved from ground zero to a spot that's closer to your goal. Maybe you've reached the midpoint of your journey; maybe you're three quarters of the way there. In fact, maybe you're just about where you want to be. Whatever the specific spot you've reached, the fact that you've already *prepared*, *organized*, and done the *work* means that you've navigated through many difficulties and completed the greater part of the journey.
- **Compare what you've accomplished to the goals that you're seeking to achieve.** Think back to the goals, both short-term and long-term, that you're seeking to accomplish. How closely does what you've done match what you're aiming to do? Zero in especially on your short-term goal for the task, and see how close you've come.
- **Evaluate your accomplishments as if you were a critical teacher from your past.** Have an out-of-body experience: Shed your old body and mind and take over the body and mind of a critical, hard-to-please teacher from your past. If you've written a paper, reread it from the perspective of that teacher. If you've studied for a test, think about the kinds of questions that teacher would ask on the test and consider whether you could answer them.
- **Evaluate what you've done as if you were your current teacher.** Now exchange bodies and minds again. This time, consider what you're doing from the perspective of your current course instructor, the one who gave you the assignment that you're evaluating. How would the instructor react to what you've done? Have you followed the assignment to the letter?

Can you figure out which aspects of your product are particularly important? Is there anything you've missed?

- **Evaluate what you've accomplished against your own standards.** Returning to your own body and mind, consider what you've done from your own perspective. How well does what you've done meet your own personal standards? Is it your best work? Do you feel confident? Have you achieved your short-term goals in the assignment? Is the product consistent with your long-term goals?

- **Be fair to yourself.** The guidelines for evaluation will help you to determine just how much further work is necessary and, even more important, *what* work is necessary. But don't go too far: It's as counterproductive to be too hard on yourself as it is to be too easy. Stick to a middle ground, always keeping your final goal in mind.

- **Based on your evaluation, revise your work.** If you're honest with yourself, it's unlikely that your first work will satisfy you. None of us can produce our best work initially. So it's necessary to return to the *work* phase of P.O.W.E.R. Learning and revise what you've done. But don't think of it as a step back: Revisions you make as a consequence of your evaluation bring you closer to your final goal.

Try It! #4
Why I Registered for Introductory Psychology

Suppose your instructor asked you to write a paragraph stating the major reasons behind your decision to enroll in Introductory Psychology. Write that paragraph below.

_____
_____
_____
_____
_____
_____
_____
_____
_____
_____

Using the evaluation criteria we've discussed, state what aspects of the paragraph fall short, and which are already acceptable.

_____
_____
_____
_____
_____
_____

Rethink

Potato chip makers had a problem: The traditional cellophane packaging they used took up too much space in warehouses and on supermarket shelves, greatly adding to their costs. On the other hand, packaging chips more tightly led to breakage and crumbling.

It wasn't until one manufacturer turned to nature that it found a solution. Specifically, someone rethinking the problem noticed that dry leaves that had fallen from trees shared many characteristics with potato chips. Like potato chips, dry leaves crumble when pressed together, and they're even similar in size and shape to potato chips. But an even more interesting characteristic of dry leaves lent itself to the potato chip problem: Leaves that are initially moistened can be packed together tightly, and after they dry they are less apt to crumble.

A solution to the potato chip problem was at hand: The manufacturer first moistened the chips and then cut them into uniform shapes. The resulting chips could be neatly stacked in compact packages. The end result—Pringle's potato chips—revolutionized the potato chip industry.

The chip innovation exemplifies rethinking, the final step in P.O.W.E.R. Learning. To *rethink* what you've accomplished earlier means to bring a fresh eye to what you've done. Use these steps to rethink what you've finished:

- **Take a fresh look at what you've done.** Review the path that you've followed, considering the choices you've made. Are you satisfied with what you've done?

- **Consider alternatives rejected earlier.** You've likely discarded possible strategies and approaches in completing your task. Now's the time to think about those approaches once more and determine if they might have been more appropriate than the road you've followed. It's still not too late to change course.

- **Follow your gut feelings.** Are you happy with what you've done? Do you feel you've gone as far as you can? Would another hour of study for a test be a good idea, or do you honestly feel you've studied as much as you can? Did you truly evaluate your work objectively, or is there still doubt in your mind?

- **Know that there's always another day.** Your future success does not depend on any single assignment, paper, or test. Don't fall victim to self-defeating thoughts such as "If I don't do well, I'll never graduate" or "Everything is riding on this one assignment." Nonsense. There is almost always an opportunity to recover from a failure.

- **Realize that deciding when to stop work is often as hard as getting started on it.** For some students, knowing when "enough is enough" is as hard as taking the initial first step on an assignment. If you've carefully evaluated what you've done and seen that there's a close fit between your goals and your work, it's time to stop work and move on.

WEB P.O.W.E.R.

The following sites on the World Wide Web provide the opportunity to extend your learning about the material in this chapter:

Adjusting to College
1) http://www.gu.edu.au/gwis/stubod/stuadv/stu_advice.html
Provides information on a variety of useful topics regarding adjusting to college life. It covers such topics as where to live, how to select classes, how to study and learn, and much more.

Psychology
2) http://www.psychology.net
This site contains loads of information relevant to psychology majors. From their "Psychology Humor Page" to reviews of graduate programs in psychology, this site has a little bit for everyone.

3) http://stange.simplenet.com/psycsite/index.htm
This site includes, among other things, links to the American Psychological Association Style Manual, tips on applying to graduate school, and listings of U.S. Psychology Ph.D. Programs.

4) http://www.apa.org
Contains useful information for psychology students regarding planing for college, graduate school, careers in psychology, and funding sources available to students of psychology.

Chapter 2

The P.O.W.E.R. Reader and Listener

It was rush hour and Arturo Greely was rushing to work along with the rest of the city, when he passed a man leaning heavily against a building. Arturo stopped and looked around. The guy didn't look too healthy. He could tell that other people could see this man and weren't stopping. He must be overreacting. The guy must be okay. Even if he wasn't, somebody else must have already checked on him.

As Arturo started to walk away, something clicked in his head. Last semester his social psychology professor had talked about situations like this one; situations in which individuals die surrounded by other people who could help them, but in which none do because no one feels responsible for helping the victims. Diffusion of responsibility...that's what it was called. And that was when Arturo made the choice to become involved. A good thing he did, too. Arturo's 911 call saved Dan Herder's life.

That afternoon Arturo made a second call, to his social psychology professor. He just wanted to tell his professor that he'd been listening.

Looking Ahead

We've all sat through classes only to discover at the end of the hour that we haven't really heard a word that our professor has said. Luckily for Dan Herder, though, Arturo had been paying attention to his professor's lecture on helping behavior. While most of us won't have the opportunity to save someone else's life, listening and reading effectively can save our own academic lives.

In this chapter, we'll consider ways to read and listen effectively. We'll start with reading. We'll consider how to assess your attention span, what you should do before you even start reading an assignment, and the ways of getting the most out of your reading. We'll then shift gears, moving from the written word to the spoken word. We'll look at ways of listening effectively and actively. We'll consider how you should listen, and what you should be listening for.

Reading with Understanding

In describing how the principles of P.O.W.E.R. Learning can be used to become a better reader, we'll focus on the type of reading that is typically called for in the study of psychology—text chapters, original texts, journal articles, and the like. However, the same principles will help you get more out of your recreational reading—both more benefit and more enjoyment.

Are you a slow reader? Do you plod through reading assignments, novels, and magazines, and end up feeling that you're taking far too long?

Or are you a fast reader? Do you whip through chapters, devour books, and fly through the daily newspaper?

Before going any further, think about your own **reading style**—your characteristic way of approaching reading tasks—by completing the In My Own Words journal.

In My Own Words
How I Read

Reflect on how you read by answering these questions.

When you open a textbook you have never seen before, what do you tend to look at first? Do you read any of the materials in the front or back of the book? Do you check out the table of contents?

When you start a new textbook chapter, what do you do first?

When you open a new paperback or magazine that you're reading for pleasure, what do you do first?

Are your reading habits the same or different for "pleasure reading" versus "assignment reading"?

When a passage that you're reading has long foreign names, what do you do? What do you do when you encounter words you don't understand?

What do you do when something you're reading makes absolutely no sense to you?

When faced with a textbook chapter that looks like it's going to be hard, what do you do? Do you ever skim through the chapter or look at the section headings or illustrations?

When you take a test that involves reading long passages, what do you do? Do you ever read the questions first, or do you start with the passage? Do your habits differ depending on the type of test? What differences do you notice?

When a reading passage seems too difficult, do you ever start to panic? Then what do you do?

Prepare: Approaching the Written Word

Preparation to begin reading isn't hard, and it won't take very long, but it's a crucial step. Your aim in preparation is to create a set of advance organizers regarding the material you're planning to read. As we discussed in Chapter 1, **advance organizers** are broad, general ideas related to new material. Advance organizers pave the way for subsequent learning, and ultimately they can help us recall material better after we've read it.

Decide on your strategy. Before you begin an assignment, think about what your goal is. Will you be reading a basic textbook on which you'll be thoroughly tested? Is your reading supposed to provide background information that will serve as a context for future learning, but that isn't essential to your success in the course? Is the material going to be useful to you personally? Realistically, how much time can you devote to the reading assignment?

The way you answer questions about your goal for reading will help you determine the strategy to adopt for reading. You aren't expected to read everything with the same degree of intensity. Some material you may feel comfortable skimming; for other material you'll want to put in the maximum effort.

Read the frontmatter of the book. If you'll be using a book extensively throughout the term, start by reading the preface and/or introduction and scanning the table of contents—what publishers call the "**frontmatter**." Instructors often don't formally assign the frontmatter, but reading it can be a big help in determining what the book's author considers important—and hence what should be important to you. The information you obtain from the frontmatter will provide a mental "hook" on which you can hang the new ideas to which you'll be exposed.

Create advance organizers. To create advance organizers, skim through the table of contents of the material you're preparing to read. Textbooks often have chapter outlines, listing the key topics to be covered, and these also can provide a way of previewing the chapter content. Think about what you already know about the topic, and how the new material in the book may relate to what you know. Consider how understanding this material will relate to your long-term goals.

You should also take a look at any end-of-chapter summaries. By reading the chapter summary—even though you haven't read the chapter yet and the summary might not make complete sense to you—you'll get a good idea of what the author considers important and will cover.

Advance organizers can also be deduced from what your course instructor says about the chapter or its topic. Sometimes instructors will mention things to pay particular attention to or to look for. Sometimes they will say why they assigned a reading. Such information provides clues that can help develop a mental list of the key ideas relating to the chapter.

Whatever you use to construct them, the crucial feature of advance organizers is to provide a framework and context for what you'll be reading. And having a framework and context can spell the difference between fully comprehending what you read and misunderstanding it. Before you proceed any further in, take this opportunity to complete the *Try It!* exercise on the next page and create an advance organizer for this chapter.

Organize: Tools of the Trade

It's obvious that the primary item you'll need to complete a reading assignment is the material that you're reading. But there are other essential tools you should gather to organize yourself, potentially including the following:

- A pencil or pen to write notes in the margin.
- A highlighter to indicate key passages in the text.
- A copy of the assignment, so you'll be sure to read the right material.
- A pad of paper and/or index cards for note-taking if the material is particularly complex. If you routinely use a word processor to take notes, get it ready.
- A dictionary. You never know what new words you'll encounter while you're reading, and a dictionary is the reference tool of choice.

Try It! #1
Create an Advance Organizer

Use any information you have available to create an advance organizer for this chapter. Feel free to return to the frontmatter, skim the section headings, or recall anything your instructor may have said about the chapter.

As you come across words, phrases, or ideas that seem unfamiliar or incomprehensible, it may be helpful to think of several questions you would ask the author if you had the opportunity. Complete the following statements to prepare your organizer:

The key topics that will be covered in the rest of this chapter are:

I think I will be most interested in:

I think I will be least interested in:

I hope the chapter covers this topic:

Words, phrases, and ideas that are unfamiliar to me include:

If the author were here, I would ask:

_____

Note: You may want to use this *Try It!* as a starting point for advance organizers for each chapter in this book.

Give yourself time. There's one more thing you need to prepare successfully for a reading assignment: enough time to complete it.

The length of reading assignments is almost never ambiguous. Instead, your reading assignment will typically be expressed as a specific page range, so you will know just how much material you will need to cover. When calculating how many pages you will have to read, remember to count the first and last pages in the range; for example, the assignment to "read pages 10 to 20" is an 11-page reading assignment, not a 10-page assignment.

Now get a watch and time yourself as you read one full page of your assignment, being sure to pay attention. Try to pick a typical page, not a particularly long or short one. Factor in your current reading attention span, which you can obtain from the *Try It!* exercise on the following page.

Try It! #2
Discover Your Attention Span

Have you ever been so engrossed in a book that you lost track of time and were late for an engagement? If so, it probably wasn't a textbook that you were reading. For most of us, keeping focused on assigned readings and paying attention in class are considerably harder than paying attention to nonacademic reading material and oral presentations, such as radio discussions, on topics of personal interest.

However, it is possible to increase your attention span…to read more effectively…to sustain your listening attention—even when the subject is academic. But before you work on increasing your attention span, it's important to know your starting point. Try to get an idea of the length of your current **attention span**—the length of time that attention is typically sustained—for both reading and listening by performing this exercise over the next few days.

Reading Attention Span:
1. Choose one of the textbooks that you've been assigned to read this semester.
2. Start reading a chapter, without any preparation, noting the time that you start reading.
3. As soon as your mind begins to wander and think about other subjects, stop reading and note the time on the chart below. Do the same thing five times over the course of a day or two. The times represent your reading attention span.

Reading Attention Span:
Trial #1____minutes Trial #2____minutes Trial #3____minutes
Trial #4____minutes Trial #5____minutes

Listening Attention Span:
1. Now carry out a similar exercise to gauge your listening attention span. Choose one of the classes you are taking this semester.
2. Note the time of the start of class, when the instructor begins speaking.
3. When your mind begins to wander, note the time. Do the same thing five times, again over a period of a few days. These times represent measures of your listening attention span.

Listening Attention Span:
Trial #1____minutes Trial #2____minutes Trial #3____minutes
Trial #4____minutes Trial #5____minutes

Ask yourself these questions about your reading and listening attention span.

1. What are your average reading and listening attention spans? (Add up the 5 numbers in each category and divide each total by 5.)
2. Is your average reading attention span different from your average listening attention span? If so, why do you think this might be?
3. Does any number in either set of trials stand out from the other numbers? For instance, is any number much higher or lower than the average? If so, can you account for this?
4. Do the numbers in your trials in either reading or listening show any trend? For instance, did your attention span tend to increase slightly over the course of the trials, did it decrease, or did it stay about the same? Can you explain any trend you may have noted?
5. Do you think your attention span figures would be very different if you had chosen a different textbook or a different class? Why?

Use the three pieces of information you now have—the length of the assignment, your per-page reading speed at full attention, and your typical attention span—to figure out roughly how long it will take you to complete the assignment. Multiply the number of pages in the assignment (e.g., 12 pages) by your per-page reading speed (e.g., 4 minutes per page) to get a full-attention reading time figure (in this example, 48 minutes). Then, if your average reading attention span is 3 minutes, figure that you will become distracted 16 times during your reading (i.e., 48 minutes divided by 3), and add in another minute or so per distraction to "recover" from the distraction. This would yield a total estimated reading time, adjusted for distractions, of 64 minutes, or 1 hour and 4 minutes.

Remember, this may sound precise but it is really only a very rough guide. In addition to distractions, you may need to interrupt your reading to look up words in the dictionary, get a drink, stretch, answer the phone, or do any of a number of other things. You may also decide to break your reading into several sessions, in which case your total reading time may be greater, since you will have to "reenter" the reading assignment each time you sit down again. Finally, as you begin to use the techniques in this chapter regularly, your reading attention span should increase, which will change your calculation.

Try It! #3
Complete a Reading Time Worksheet

Use the process described above to calculate the approximate time it will take you to complete a textbook reading assignment you have been given. (Using this book may not be a good idea, since your reading will be broken up intentionally by frequent built-in "distractions," such as this *Try It!* exercise.) Then compare your prediction with the time it actually takes you to complete the assignment.

Use the worksheet below:

A.   Total length of reading assignment =

B.   Time required to read one page at full attention =

C.   Full-attention reading time, in minutes (A x B) =

D.   Average reading attention span (calculated earlier) =

E.   Estimated number of interruptions due to attention lapses =

F.   Assuming one minute per interruption, total estimated reading time required (C + E) =

G.   Actual reading time (fill in after completing the assignment) =

Work: The Rites of Reading

Finally, it's time to get down to work and start reading.

Obviously—because it's what you're doing at this very moment—you know how to read. But what's important is what you do *while* you're reading. Here are several things that will help you get the most out of the process of reading:

Stay focused. Your job is to keep distracting thoughts at bay and focus on the material you are supposed to be reading. It's not easy, but there are things you can do to help yourself stay focused:

- **Read in small bites.** If you've figured it is going to take you four hours to read an entire chapter, break up the four hours into more manageable time periods. Promise yourself that you'll read for one hour in the afternoon, another hour in the evening, and the next two hours spaced out during the following day. One hour of reading is far more manageable than a four-hour block. Even within the smaller periods, set times when you'll take a break—say, every half hour.

- **Take a break.** Actually, plan to take several breaks to reward yourself while you're reading. During your break, do something enjoyable—eat a snack, watch a bit of a ball game on television, play a video game, or the like. Just try not to get drawn in to your break activity to the point that it takes over your reading time.
- **Deal with distractions.** Sometimes problems have a way of popping into our minds and repeatedly distracting us. If a particular problem keeps interrupting your concentration— such as a difficulty you're having on the job—try to think of an action-oriented strategy to deal with it. You might even write your proposed solution down on a piece of paper. That can move the problem out of the mental realm of your head and put it into concrete form on paper, potentially making it less intrusive.

<u>Write while you read.</u> Writing is one of the most important aspects of reading. If you haven't underlined, jotted notes to yourself, placed check marks on the page, drawn arrows, constructed diagrams, and otherwise defaced and disfigured your book while you're reading, you're not doing your job as a P.O.W.E.R. Reader.

What, exactly, should you be writing while you are reading? There are several things you should write down:

- **Rephrase key points.** Make notes to yourself, in your own words, about what the author is trying to get across. Don't just copy what's been said. Think about the material, and rewrite it in words that are your own.

    Writing notes to yourself in your own words has several consequences, all good. First, you take ownership of the material by transforming it into your words. It becomes something you now understand and is part of your own personal knowledge base.

    Second, trying to summarize a key point in your own words will reveal with absolute clarity whether you truly understand it. It's easy to be fooled into thinking we understand something as we're reading along. But the true test is whether we can explain it to ourselves (or someone else), using our own vocabulary.

    Third, the very act of writing engages an additional type of perception—involving the kinesthetic sense of moving a pen or pressing a keyboard. Engagement of an additional perceptual system will help you learn the material in a more active way.

    Finally, writing notes and phrases will help you study the material later. Not only will the key points be highlighted, but your notes will quickly bring you up to speed regarding what you were thinking about initially.

- **Highlight or underline key points.** Very often the first or last sentence in a paragraph, or the first or last paragraph in a section, will present a key point. (Remember those lessons about "topic sentences" you had in high school English classes? Writers really use them.)

    Before you highlight anything, though, read the whole paragraph through. Then you'll be sure that what you highlight is, in fact, the key information. Topic sentences do not always fall at the beginning of a paragraph.

    It's also important to be judicious in your highlighting and underlining. A page covered in yellow highlighter is artistically appealing, but it won't help you understand the material any better. *In highlighting and underlining, less is more.* One rule of thumb: No more than 10 percent of the material should be highlighted or underlined.

- **Use arrows, diagrams, outlines, tables, timelines, charts, and other visuals to help you understand and later recall what you are reading.** If there are three examples given for an assertion, number them. If a paragraph discusses a situation in which an earlier point does not hold, link the original point to the exception by an arrow. If a sequence of steps is presented, number each step.

Representing the material graphically permits you to think about it in new and different ways. Rather than considering the material solely in verbal terms, you now add visual images. Not only will the act of creating a diagram help you to understand the material better, it will ease its later recall. In fact, a mental picture of a page on which you've graphically linked up ideas might leap into your head while you're taking a test.

Evaluate: Appraising the Message

Evaluation is a crucial step in reading. At the most basic level, you need to be able to answer a disarmingly simple question: "What does all this mean?"

But there's another aspect to evaluation. You need to evaluate, truthfully and honestly, your own level of understanding. Evaluation, then, consists of the following steps:

- **Identify the value of the main ideas and themes *to you personally*.** Try to determine the take-home message of the material you've read. Sometimes it is spelled out, and at other times you will have to deduce it for yourself.
- **Prioritize the ideas.** Of all the information that is presented, which is the most crucial to the main message, and which is the least crucial? Make a list of the main topics covered, and try to rank them in order of importance.
- **Think critically about the arguments.** Do they hold together? Are the author's assertions reasonable? Are there any flaws in the arguments? Would authors with a different point of view dispute what is being said? What other perspectives might the author have taken?
- **Assess your own level of understanding.** The most reliable way to see how well you understand material is to try to teach it to someone else.

  If you have a willing roommate or friend, talk through the material, explaining the difficult concepts. Try to do it without referring to the chapter itself, but make sure you cover all of the material you've read. If you can discuss the material in a way that a person unfamiliar with the chapter can understand, you've made significant progress in mastering the material.
- **Talk to yourself—out loud!—about the material.** This is one time when talking out loud when no one is around is not only normal, but beneficial. Summarize the material aloud, as if you were talking to another person.

  Talking out loud does two things. First, it helps you identify weak spots in your understanding. Talking to yourself will help you nail down concepts that are still not clear in your own mind. Second, and equally important, because you are transforming the written word into the spoken word, you are using another modality to think about the information. Later, when you try to recall it, the additional modality will help you remember more effectively.
- **Be honest with yourself.** Most of us are able to read with our minds on cruise control. But the net result is not much different from not reading the passage at all. If you have drifted off while you've been reading, go back and reread the passage.
- **Pat yourself on the back and take a bow.** Just as you've done during each of your reading breaks, reward yourself for completing the reading passage. But keep in mind there's one more step before you can really relax, and it's a crucial one: rethinking what you've read.

Rethink: Getting It the Second Time

You're human, so—like the rest of us—you'd probably like nothing more than to heave a sigh of relief and, at least temporarily, push what you've read out of your mind.

Not yet. There's a crucial step you should take that will assist you in cementing what you've learned into memory: rethinking what you've read. If you do it within 24 hours of first reading the assignment, it can save you hours of work later.

The best way to rethink an assignment is to reread it, along with any notes you've taken. "Ouch," you're probably thinking. "I just did that." True, but the benefits of rereading can't be overstated. Rereading transfers material from your short-term memory to your long-term memory. It solidifies information so that it will be remembered far better over the long haul.

The good news is that rereading will take far less time than it did the first time. In fact, it isn't even necessary to read word-for-word. You already know what's important and what's not important, so you can skim some of the less important material. But it is wise to reread the more important material carefully, making sure that you fully understand what is being discussed and why.

Rethinking should be the central activity as you reread the passage and your notes. You need to be sure that your understanding is complete and that you're able to answer any questions that you earlier had about the material.

<u>The concept map as a rethinking tool.</u> Most of us are familiar with outlining, which involves the use of numbers and letters to depict the structure of a body of written material. There's another tool sometimes used by readers—and writers too—to organize the thoughts expressed in writing. Many people find it easier and more intuitive than outlining. It is called concept mapping.

Basically, **concept mapping** is a method of structuring written material by graphically grouping and connecting key ideas and themes. Each key idea is placed in a different part of the map, and related ideas are placed near it—above, below, or beside it. What emerges does not have the rigid structure of an outline. Instead, a "finished" concept map looks something like a map of the solar system, with the largest and most central idea in the center (the "Sun" position), and related ideas surrounding it at various distances. It has also been compared to a large tree, with numerous branches and subbranches radiating out from a central trunk.

The main advantages of a concept map are that it is free, open, and expandable. Ideas and details can be added to the map as they are encountered or reviewed in reading, and connecting lines can be drawn to link related ideas. The resulting structure—which is especially useful for rethinking and review—evolves as the reader fills in ideas and places them on the map.

Look at the following page for an example of a concept map of the first half of this chapter, on reading. You will be asked in a later *Try It!* to draw a concept map of your own to summarize the key ideas and relationships of the second half of this chapter, on listening.

You should note that concept mapping, also known as semantic mapping, originated as a writing tool. Before drafting essays, people would jot down related ideas to serve as the main points and supporting details for a series of paragraphs. You may want to try it in your writing as well as your reading.

Listening with Understanding

Consider these basic two facts: When we speak, most of us talk at a rate of around 125 words a minute. But the average listener can comprehend close to 700 words per minute.

Then why is it so hard to listen closely to what someone is saying? Why do our minds wander, and why do we often recall so little about a class when it is over?

The answer rests on the difference between *hearing* and *listening*. Although our sensory capabilities permit us to *hear* far more words than are produced in a given minute by the average speaker, that doesn't mean we actively *listen* to speech. **Hearing** is the involuntary act of sensing sounds. In fact, even when we wish to avoid hearing something, we're sometimes prisoners of our sense of hearing. The annoying drip of a faucet or the grating sound of a roommate's voice speaking on the phone in the next room may make us weary, but what we're hearing has little or no meaning.

Concept Map
Reading with Understanding

ORGANIZE
Tools
Time!

WORK
Focus:
    bites
    breaks
    deal with distractions
<u>Write</u> while reading
    rephrase
    highlight
    arrows, lines, etc.
    mark up the page!

PREPARE
Advance organizers
Strategy: goal
    intensity
Frontmatter

READING WITH
UNDERSTANDING

Reading style
Speed
    unimportant
    understanding matters!
Attention span

RETHINK
Reread
(skim)

EVALUATE
Personal value of ideas
Prioritize ideas
Think critically (Do I agree?)
Teach someone else
Talk out loud
Honesty!

In contrast, **listening** is the voluntary act of focusing on what is being said, making sense of it, and thinking about it in a way that permits it to be recalled accurately. Listening involves concentration. And it requires shutting out competing thoughts, such as what we need to pick up at the grocery store or why our date last night was so terrific.

In the classroom, listening with understanding is essential. Active listening will help you understand class presentations better. It will aid you in mastering material, permit you to participate more in class, and help you work with your classmates more effectively.

In My Own Words
How I Listen

Reflect on how you listen. Your reflection should address both "external" factors relating to the speaker, topic, setting, and occasion, as well as "internal" factors relating to your mood, attitude, habits, preferences, and receptivity. Now complete these items.

I find myself "drifting off" instead of listening whenever:

I find myself listening attentively whenever:

What are the key differences between the times when you drift off and the times when you listen attentively?

Which differences reside in *you* rather than in external factors?

How would you define active listening?

Can you think of any ways to change your listening habits to decrease your "drifting off" experiences?

The key to effective listening involves approaching the process systematically. Even if you have trouble staying focused on a boring lecturer, following the basic procedures of the P.O.W.E.R. system can help you get the most out of your experience.

Prepare: Getting Warmed Up

Preparing for a lecture is like working out before an athletic event. You need to get yourself into shape by anticipating what you will have to do and readying your body for the event. Preparing for actively listening to a class lecture involves readying your mind through the following steps:

- **Read your notes from the previous class session.** Instructors generally pick up where they left off during the previous class and may not review the material. Your own review of the material will permit you to be fully up-to-speed when the lecture starts.
- **Do all reading assigned for the class.** A lecture may be explicitly designed to answer questions about the reading, or it may use the reading as a launching point for the presentation of new material. You'll be at a huge disadvantage in understanding what is going on if you haven't completed the assigned readings before coming to class.
- **Think about what will probably be covered in class.** You may not know for sure what your instructor plans to cover in the upcoming class, but you probably can get a general idea by looking at the syllabus or by recalling what was discussed at the end of the previous class.

Organize: Creating a Listening Space

Your next step is to organize your "listening space" for most effective listening. Use your knowledge of yourself—of what works best for you—to get your mind and body ready for active listening. Here are some suggestions.

- **Organize what you need to listen effectively.** Taking notes will require pen, paper, and notebooks, and you should come to class with them. If the instructor often refers to the course textbook, make sure you've brought the book to class. It's also important to come to class with the course syllabus, because assignments and test dates may change and you'll want to be able to jot down the most recent information.
- **Choose a classroom seat that will promote active listening.** You should certainly choose a seat that will permit your to see and hear clearly, but there's more to it than that.

  What's the best place to sit? Usually it's near the front center of the classroom. Instructors make more eye contact with the people near them, and they sometimes believe that the best, most engaged students sit closest. Conversely, they may assume that students who sit as far toward the back of the room as they can get are less involved. (There's a certain reality to that assumption: Research shows that more questions are asked by students sitting close to instructors than those further back.)

  Furthermore, sitting in the back of the class may make you feel disengaged and out of touch with what is happening at the front of the room. In turn, this may make it easier for your mind to wander.

  But everyone needs to make a personal choice about what works best. If you feel as if you're on display in the front of the class and sitting there inhibits your asking questions, then choose a different seat.

Work: Finding the Right Focus

Listening can be a totally passive process. You can sit back and let the voice of the instructor wash over you, and leave a class knowing no more than when you first entered it. But if you actively listen, you'll be constantly aware of what the instructor and your classmates are saying, interpreting it and shaping it to be maximally useful to you. Here is what you need to do to be an effective listener:

- **Focus on what is being said.** In essence, successful listening involves paying attention to two kinds of messages: the actual message and what's called the meta-message. The actual message consists of the verbatim transcript; it is what the speaker actually says, on a surface level. But all speakers also have a **meta-message**, the underlying main ideas that they seek to convey through the spoken message.

  Sometimes a speaker will explicitly state the meta-message. For example, an instructor might say at the start of a class, "Today I'll be trying to give you a feel for the ways that social psychologists approach the problem of group violence." In other cases, though, the meta-message may not be so obviously stated, and listeners will have to figure out the underlying themes.

- **Pay attention to the nonverbal messages that accompany the verbal message.** Does an instructor get excited about a particular topic? Does he or she get agitated? Does the speaker seem unenthusiastic when talking about something? Use nonverbal cues to gauge the importance of a particular part of a message relative to other things being said.
- **Listen for what is *not* being said.** Sometimes silence is not just golden, but informative as well. By noting what topics are *not* being covered in class, or are presented only minimally, we can gauge the relative importance of ideas in comparison to one another.

  This is where careful preparation comes in. Only if you have done the assigned readings in advance will you be able to gauge which topics are being particularly emphasized and which are not discussed at all. This information is important. It will help you get a good sense of an instructor's priorities and help you later when the time comes to study for exams.
- **Take notes.** As you no doubt know from experience, no one's memory is infallible. Unless you take careful and accurate notes, you're likely to end up with little or even no recollection of the details of a speaker's message. In later chapters, we'll be discussing memory and notetaking in detail. For now, keep in mind that taking notes will aid active listening by helping you to focus on the speaker's message.

Evaluate: What Did You Say?

Your evaluation of what you are hearing should begin while you are listening and continue after. Specifically, here are several ways of evaluating what you are hearing:
- **Evaluate your level of understanding.** One of the hardest tasks we face is assessing just how much we truly comprehend. Be honest with yourself, asking, "Do I really comprehend this material?" For example, if a lecturer has just outlined the way to calculate the numerical mean of a group of scores, you should evaluate whether you could figure out the mean yourself if you were asked to. (Remember, you *will* be asked to do it at some point.)
- **Think critically about what is being said.** Adopt a questioning attitude, in which your goal is not passive acceptance but active evaluation. Do you agree with the speaker? Do you understand the reasoning behind the speaker's arguments? Are the arguments logical? Is this information consistent with other material that's been presented earlier?
- **Ask questions.** One of the most important things you can do during class is to ask questions. Raising questions will help you evaluate, clarify, and ultimately better understand what your instructor is saying. Even beyond these critical goals, questions serve several other purposes.

  For one thing, raising questions will help you to personalize the material being covered, permitting you to draw it more closely into your own framework and perspective. Furthermore, when you ask a question and it is answered satisfactorily, you become personally engaged with what the instructor is saying.

  Questioning also increases your involvement in the class as a whole. If you sit back and never raise questions in class, you are much less likely to feel a real part of the class. Becoming an active questioner will rightly make you feel like you have contributed something to the class. Remember, if you are unclear about some point, it is likely that others share your lack of clarity.

  Finally, by asking questions in class, you serve as a role model for other students. Your questions may help break the ice in a class, making it easier for others to raise issues that they have about the material. And ultimately the answers that the instructor provides to *others'* questions may help *you* to better understand and evaluate your understanding of the material.

Rethink: Giving Yourself a Grade in Listening

Have you ever attended a lecture and find the next day that you have only the foggiest notion of what the speaker said? One way to avoid that kind of feeling is to *rethink* what you've heard.

To rethink the speaker's message, analyze what the speaker said. Consider the underlying goals that the speaker must have had for the presentation—what he or she was attempting to achieve. Think about the *way* the message was presented and how that effected your evaluation of it. If the speaker was attempting to persuade you in some way, what arguments were most effective? Which fell short? Were you influenced by the speaker's style—his or her nonverbal behavior, intonation, and delivery—instead of the content of the message? If you were influenced by such irrelevant factors, can you separate out the content and think of it independently? Can the speaker's arguments be recast in a different light to lead to a different conclusion?

Finally, rethinking involves considering your own behavior. How effectively did you listen? Did you listen attentively, or were there periods during which you "spaced out" on what was being said? If there were, what can you do to recapture what you may have missed?

In short, active listening does not end in the moment of silence that follows the end of a class or lecture or conversation. It needs to continue, as you rethink the meaning of the message.

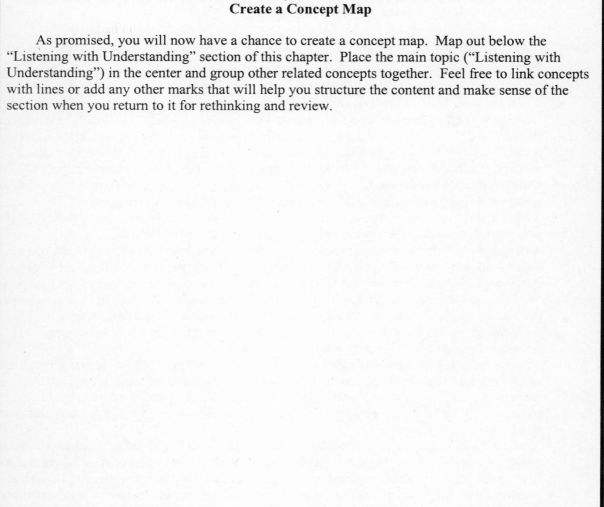

Try It! #4
Create a Concept Map

As promised, you will now have a chance to create a concept map. Map out below the "Listening with Understanding" section of this chapter. Place the main topic ("Listening with Understanding") in the center and group other related concepts together. Feel free to link concepts with lines or add any other marks that will help you structure the content and make sense of the section when you return to it for rethinking and review.

WEB P.O.W.E.R.

Reading Strategies

1) http://www.schooledu.sut.edu/Dev.ed/PLAN/PLAN_teach

Provides a useful study-reading strategy that is demonstrated on an actual college text.

Classic Readings in Psychology

2) http://www.yorku.ca/dept/psych/classics

A collection of historically significant writings related to the field of psychology.

Effective Listening

3) http://www1.geocities.com/SiliconValley?Pines/1814/essay514.htm

One of the best ways to improve your listening ability is to be aware of the obstacles to effective listening. This site describes several common obstacles to effective listening.

4) http://www.cpcc.cc.nc.us/instructional/studytips/EffectiveList.htm

This site presents a quick-tip guide to better listening skills. The habits of good and bad listeners associated with each tip are described.

Chapter 3

The P.O.W.E.R. Writer and Speaker

On the first day of his developmental psychology class Mike Jacobs sat in his seat with butterflies beginning to stir in his stomach. His professor was reading through the syllabus—the class sounded great, just what he'd hoped it would be. Mike had a younger brother with multiple sclerosis and had always wanted to work with physically and mentally challenged children. This class was a requirement for the minor in developmental disabilities.

Unfortunately, his professor had just gotten to the portion of the syllabus that detailed the assignments for the class. Mike could handle the two exams—no problem. The 15-page final paper and 10-minute oral presentation were another story, though. He didn't know which part of the assignment terrified him more. He'd never been a particularly good writer, and speaking in public scared him practically to death.

"I'm in college now," he thought to himself. "I could just drop this class and take something else. That would be much easier. I really want to work with kids, though. Is it worth giving that up just because of a paper and an oral report? Somehow I'll have to get through this."

Looking Ahead

As psychology students you will probably not be able to escape written assignments and oral presentations, even if those oral presentations are simply in the form of stating your opinion in class. Because they are so important, writing and speaking present extraordinary challenges. Few activities raise so many anxieties, but few are so important to our ultimate success.

This chapter focuses on writing and speaking. We begin by considering the ways to write a college-level paper. We consider how to get started writing a paper and how to choose a goal and audience for it. We discuss the different sections of a paper and how to move from a rough first draft to a final draft of which you can be proud.

While studying psychology, you will, at some point, be asked to conduct and write-up research. These types of research papers have a very specific format and we have included a list of web sites and books at the end of this chapter that deal specifically with experimental research papers. Although we focus on general research-oriented reports, many of the approaches we discuss apply to this type of writing as well.

The remainder of the chapter looks at oral presentations. We discuss ways to engage our listeners from the very start of our talk. We consider the importance of practicing neither too little nor too much. We also look at ways of dealing with our anxieties about speaking.

P.O.W.E.R. Writing

Writing is not easy, and for many students, writing assignments raise more anxieties than virtually any other academic task. These anxieties may be the result of prior unhappy experiences that we've had with writing. Or it may be that we've never really been taught how to write. Or perhaps we're convinced that we simply don't have the knack of writing well, that there's a special writing gene, and we just weren't born with it.

In My Own Words
How I Feel about Writing

Reflect on the feelings you have about writing.

When I receive a writing assignment, my initial reaction is:

I prepare for writing assignments by:

Compared to other students I know, my writing is:

Do you ever write for pleasure? When? Under what circumstances?

Do you ever spontaneously take out a piece of paper when called upon to explain something? Under what circumstances?

Are you a note-taker? A doodler and scribbler?

Which writing experiences are particularly pleasant for you? Which are unpleasant?

What tools do you need to gather when preparing for a lengthy writing assignment? Do you have special pencils or pens? A favorite chair? Do you prefer to use a computer?

Are you particularly good at finding ways to put off writing tasks? Do you do anything to prevent this?

When faced with a lengthy writing assignment, how do you decide what to write? How do you organize your thoughts?

Do you make a habit of reviewing and rewriting, or would you rather stay with your first draft and be done with it?

When you take a test that involves writing, such as an essay test, what do you do? Do you outline your responses? Do you do anything to gather your ideas? Do your habits differ depending on the type of test? What differences do you notice?

When a writing assignment seems too difficult, do you ever start to panic? Then what do you do?

Delete from your memory bank any negative preconceptions you may have about writing. There is no mystery to writing; it's a skill that can be taught, and a skill that, with practice, anybody can learn.

This chapter presents a strategy, based on the P.O.W.E.R. Learning system, that will help you achieve the goal of writing clearly and competently. It will help you to build upon your strengths and maximize your abilities. It will permit you to express your inner thoughts, translating what's inside your head into words that allow others to understand you in a way that approximates what you yourself are experiencing.

Prepare: Confronting the Blank Page

There is nothing more intimidating than a blank piece of paper. Nothing. It is something that every writer faces, no matter how proficient. Plato, Shakespeare, Elizabeth Barrett Browning, Malcolm X, Toni Morrison. Each them felt the terror of having to fill that white blankness with words.

Looked at another way, though, there is nothing more liberating than a blank page. It offers every possibility, and it gives you the freedom to say whatever you want to say. And therein lies the key to good writing: deciding what it is you want to say.

Preparation is the central aspect of successful writing. Writing is a process, and preparation for it encompasses the following steps:

Determine your goal. To write successfully, you need to think about the end product. If there is a choice among different types of writing, decide which will make you most comfortable. If one choice is to prepare an essay, and you are creative and enjoy expressing your opinions, choose that option. If you enjoy amassing a set of facts and drawing a conclusion from them, a research paper might well be the best choice.

Once you've nailed down the specific type of writing you are going to do, the next step is to choose a topic. Although instructors usually assign a particular topic, in some cases the choice will be left to you.

But the freedom to choose a topic does not come without a price. In fact, many students find that choosing what to write about is harder than actually writing the paper itself. Here are some things you can do to help pick an appropriate topic:

- **Use "freewriting."** According to Peter Elbow, a writing expert who has revolutionized the teaching of writing, one of the reasons we find writing so hard is that we have a set of censors inside our heads.[1] At a moment's notice, those censors are ready to spring up and whisper, "That's no good," when we set pen to paper.

    However, there is a way to keep these internal voices at bay. You can use a technique called "freewriting." In **freewriting**, you write continuously for a fixed period of time, such as five or ten minutes. The only rule that governs freewriting is to write continuously, without stopping. It doesn't matter if the product is bad; it doesn't matter if it's good. The only principle you must follow in freewriting is to get something—anything—down on paper.

Try it, and you'll see how liberating freewriting can be. Of course the product will not be perfect, but you'll find that you've most likely written something of value. You've probably thought of some new ideas, new approaches, or new strategies that will help you to decide on a topic. What's more, you've probably formed an "attitude" toward one or more potential topics, which can be used to add a personal voice and authenticity to your writing.

Once the freewriting session is completed, you may want to write a single sentence that captures the main point of what you have written—the "center of gravity," Elbow calls it. You can then use this sentence as a springboard for further exploration of ideas the next time you write.

- **Use brainstorming.** The oral equivalent of freewriting is brainstorming. In **brainstorming**, you say out loud as many ideas as you can think of in a fixed period of time. Although brainstorming works best when you do it with a group of friends or classmates, you can do it by yourself. (This is one of those times when talking to yourself has its benefits.)

As with freewriting, the idea is to temporarily silence the censors that prevent us from saying whatever comes into our heads. In brainstorming, the initial goal is not to produce high-quality ideas, but a high quantity of ideas. You can revisit and evaluate the ideas you've come up with later. For now, the goal simply is to produce as many ideas as possible, no matter how implausible, silly, or irrelevant. Surprisingly enough, brainstorming, like freewriting, produces some very usable ideas.

Try It! #1
Get Your Brain Storming: Using Brainstorming to Generate Ideas

A newspaper…a light bulb…a candle. Each of these common household items has a well established, obvious use, but there are other things that you can do with them.

Try brainstorming as many additional uses as you can for each item. Remember, the idea is to produce as many possibilities as you can, without evaluating how realistic or feasible they may be. Think quantity over quality.

Newspaper:

Light bulb:

Candle:

Go back to your answers and circle each use that you think is realistic and at least theoretically possible.

Did brainstorming work? Did you surprise yourself with the number of alternative possibilities you generated for each item?

<u>Determine who your audience will be</u>. "That's easy," you may be thinking, "it's my instructor." Not so fast. Although the instructor is the most obvious reader for what you write, you should think of your audience in terms of the ultimate purpose of the writing assignment. For example, if you're writing a paper about schizophrenia, are you directing it to a layperson who knows little about the topic? Or are you writing it for someone with a good understanding of mental illness, someone who already knows about DSM-IV, neurotransmitters, and positive and negative symptoms? Clearly, the answer to these questions will make a difference in how and what you write.

In short, it's crucial to know—and to keep in mind—the persons to whom you are writing. What is their level of knowledge about the topic? Are they already predisposed to a particular position? What do you think they would like to take away with them after they read what you've written?

Keeping an audience in mind serves another purpose: It personalizes your writing. Rather than targeting your writing to a nondescript blob of individuals who are members of an indeterminate group ("all the people who might be interested in schizophrenia"), you individualize your audience. Think of the reader as your sister, or a friend, or your next-door neighbor. Think of how that individual would feel after reading what you've written, and what you would say to convince him or her. Remember, your writing is a representation of you as an individual. It means something to you, and you want its impact to be felt just as personally by another individual.

<u>Research the topic</u>. In order to write most papers, you must do research. The research process involves identifying relevant information by examining books, magazine and journal articles, and the Internet and World Wide Web. It's often a major task, and we'll consider it in detail in Chapter 6 when we discuss information management.

For now, though, keep in mind that the best way to proceed is to take notes on 3" x 5" cards. These cards can be a writer's best friend. Not only do they allow you to note, and later recall, what your research has uncovered, but you can easily sort them.

Just what should notecards contain? The key is to place no more than one major idea on each card. Sometimes that major idea will take a few words; other times it will consist of several sentences. If you avoid including more than one major idea on a card, you will find it easy later on to sort them and to place related pieces of information together.

One other important point about notecards: Make sure every notecard contains information that clearly identifies its source. We'll discuss this more in Chapter 6, but for now keep in mind that it is critical that you know where you found the idea on the notecard. Not only will this save you a lot of trouble if you need to return to the source of the idea later, but it will permit you to indicate appropriately in the paper the source of the idea.

Finally, it's critical that you write the ideas you place on the notecards in your own words. Unless you find some particularly compelling phrases that you think you might want to include in the final paper—which you should set off with quotation marks—*always* use your own words on notecards. Using your own words will prevent you from accidentally copying others' words and passing them off as your own—the gravest of academic sins. But it does something more: Rephrasing what a source has written helps ensure that you really understand it yourself.

By the way, if you are computer literate, this whole process can be done using a word processing program. Instead of notecards, place each idea in a separate paragraph, which can then be sorted and shifted around. In fact, some word processing programs have built-in features to help you organize your research.

<u>Break the task down</u>. If you have to write a 10-page paper, don't think of it as 10 pages. Instead, break it down into chunks of two pages a day, spread out over five days. Or think of it in terms of the major sections: an introduction, a description of the background of an issue, arguments in favor of a position, arguments against a position, and a conclusion. You could then schedule writing each of those five sections on a different day.

Organize: Constructing a Scaffold

When we read and listen to information, the organization phase is really pretty easy: The author or speaker has already constructed a framework for presenting the information to us. Our job as readers and listeners is to figure out what that organization is, like detectives following a trail of clues.

When we're writing, however, there is no trail to follow: We're the ones creating something that hasn't existed before. Consequently, it's up to us to come up with the scaffolding on which to place our written product.

Construct an outline. The fundamental key to organizing an extended piece of writing is the outline. Outlines provide a roadmap to follow when we're writing, a set of sequential steps that show us where we are heading and how we are going to get there.

The secret of successful outlining is flexibility: It is essential to keep an open mind about sequencing and to avoid getting "locked in" prematurely to a pattern that might later prove unworkable. The best approach is to place possible outline topics, based on your research, on 3" x 5" cards. Then read through all the cards and try to place them in a logical order. Ask yourself how the information builds up into a complete and convincing presentation. Remember your audience and treat your readers courteously. Ask yourself what a reader would have to know already in order to understand a given fact or argument. Try out several sequences, and determine which order works best.

You can do the same sort of thing on a computer screen using a word processing program. List all your topics and rearrange them to your heart's content. If you use the program's outlining feature, it will even renumber the outline as you make changes.

Organize the paper's structure. Although sometimes instructors provide a structure for a paper, you may have to construct one yourself. One way to do this is to follow the **ABBCC structure.** "ABBCC" stands for the five parts of a typical research paper: Argument, Background, Body, Counterarguments, and Conclusion. Each of these parts plays a specific role in the overall paper:

- **Argument**. Just as we introduce ourselves when we meet someone for the first time, a writer needs to introduce a reader to the main argument being put forward in the paper. Every paper should have a main argument or **thesis,** a one- or two-sentence description of the point that is being made in the paper. For instance, your thesis might make the argument that, "Violent children watch greater amounts of television than less violent children."

  A thesis should be stated as a contention ("people are their own worst enemies") or in terms of some action verb ("the recent increase in reports of repressed memories requires that more research be conducted in this area"). The best thesis statements take a stand on some controversy and include such key words as "should" or "ought." For instance, "The effects of psychological stress on physical health should be given more consideration by government health officials" presents a thesis statement; "this paper will discuss the effects of psychological stress on physical health" is simply stating the topic.

  The argument need not be the first sentence of the paper. In fact, it is usually wise to start off with something that grabs readers' attention. Begin with a controversial quote, an illustrative story, or a personal encounter—anything that is likely to make a reader sit up and take notice.

  In addition to presenting the main thesis of the paper, the argument section should lay out the areas that you will cover and the general scope of the paper. You should use this section to present the paper's overall perspective and point-of-view. However, you shouldn't provide evidence yet for why your arguments are correct; save that for the body of the paper.

- **Background.** You'll need to provide readers with a context in which to place your paper's arguments, and the background section is the place to do it. Provide a brief history of the topic, talking about different approaches that have been taken and different schools of thought. Introduce any unusual terminology you might need to employ. If the topic is highly controversial, trace the controversy, and discuss why people have found the topic so controversial.

- **Body.** The body makes up the bulk of most papers. In the paper's body, restate your thesis and provide evidence as to why the thesis is correct.

    Present the evidence in a logical order. Start with the least persuasive arguments, and move into those that are the most persuasive. Or you might start with the least controversial arguments, and move into the ones that are most debatable.

    When deciding the order in which to present information, keep your audience firmly in mind. For instance, a paper on extrasensory perception (ESP) targeted to parapsychologists might be very different from one written for a more skeptical audience.

- **Counterarguments.** Your paper is incomplete unless you touch upon information that runs counter to your own thesis. State the counterarguments to your position, and systematically refute each one. This section need not be long, but it is crucial. By acknowledging and then refuting the major counterarguments, you help reinforce your own position. And if you don't do this, you open your paper to the criticism that you didn't take opposing arguments seriously.

- **Conclusion.** A good ending to a paper is as important as a good beginning. It's your last opportunity to show readers what you know and to convince them of your point of view.

    The conclusion should summarize the thesis and the arguments that you raised earlier. This is not the place to introduce new information; all information should have been introduced earlier. Instead, recap the information and ideas in the paper. Close with a flourish. You might present an anecdote that is linked to one that you presented at the start of the paper, or you might end by posing a question. However you choose to conclude the paper, make sure that it ties the various pieces together.

Work: The Write to Work

You've reached the moment that many of us dread: It's time to actually start writing. However, if you've carefully prepared and organized, there's good news for you: Many of the hardest aspects of writing are behind you. The outline provides a clear roadmap of where you are headed, and your research notecards will permit you to flesh out the points of your outline. In fact, one way to look at your outline is that it provides you with the major headings of your paper. The job of writing the paper then becomes a matter of matching up the research to the appropriate outline heading, rather than starting with a blank sheet of paper.

Still, the work of writing is not easy. The best way to proceed is to divide the actual work of writing into two stages: writing the first draft and revising your draft.

Writing the first draft. When you set pen to paper or fingers to keyboard to begin writing, don't feel that you are carving your words in stone. Permit yourself to be less than perfect. Don't worry about word choice, grammar, sentence structure, spelling, or punctuation. That can come later. The first draft is meant to give you something to move on from. The important thing is to fill up that blank space with *something*.

What's the rationale for such an approach? The simple answer: It's considerably easier to work from an existing draft—even one that is far from perfect—than to work from nothing. In most ways, the first draft is the hardest you'll have to do, and it's important to get the process underway. By liberating yourself from the constraints of getting things perfect the first time, you will make far easier the process of translating what's in your head to a form that others can see.

There are several strategies you can use to make writing the first draft less painful:

- **Start where you like.** You need not follow the order of the outline when you write. For example, some writers start a paper by writing the conclusion section first. By keeping the end in mind, they know just where they are headed, making the journey a little easier. Similarly, other writers save the beginning of the paper for last, reasoning that they'll be better able to tell their readers where the paper is going after it has actually gotten there.

What's most important is that you start writing *something*. Write whatever part of the paper you feel most comfortable writing, because just having something on paper is a comforting feeling and will encourage you to write the rest.

- **Turn off your inner critic.** If you're anything like everyone else, with every word you write, there's probably a voice somewhere in your head that's whispering, "Terrible sentence. Dumb idea. Forget it, you idiot, you'll never finish this paper." That's the voice of your inner critic, and it's a voice that keeps many of us from reaching our potential as good writers.

  Your job is to turn that voice off, at least for now. (You'll want to use it later, when the nagging may come in handy as you revise your work.) While you're working on your first draft, you want to give yourself permission to let your creative processes put words on paper. As long as you write things down, you'll be able to go back, change things, and make your paper better. But you can't revise what isn't there.

- **Go with the flow.** When you're writing your first draft, try to write quickly. Writing often takes on a rhythm, and you should try to write in synch with the flow of that rhythm. If you're on a roll, go with it. Don't stop to edit your work; that will happen later.

  On the other hand, if you're having trouble getting into a rhythm, and each word is like pulling teeth, take a break. Do something entirely different for a few minutes and then return with a fresh mind.

  If you're really having trouble, try rearranging your notecards. You might even shuffle them (after you've first numbered them so you can go back to the original order.) Placing them in a random order may provide a fresh way of looking at your topic, and this may in turn free you enough to get your writing started.

- **Don't be afraid to modify your outline.** When you start writing, it's easy to fall into the trap of viewing an outline as a rigid, unbending framework. But this is not what an outline is. Your outline is a living document, and you should feel free to rearrange headings and even to deviate from it as you're creating your first draft. You'll have the opportunity later to check that the writing still follows a logical course.

- **Use your own voice.** Each of us has a distinct *writing* **voice**. That voice represents our own unique style, a reflection of our outlook on life and our past writing experiences.

  Avoid the temptation to write as if you were someone else. Instead, use your own natural voice and vocabulary, and don't use big words in an effort to impress your audience. If you'd feel foolish saying "heretofore" in a conversation, you shouldn't use it when you're writing a paper. Don't scan the thesaurus in search of unusual words, and don't give in to the temptation that word-processor thesauruses offer of plugging in new and unusual words for simple ones. Just because you can do something doesn't mean you should.

- **Forget about it.** The last step in creating a first draft is the easiest: Put it aside. In order to revise your draft effectively—the next step in writing—it's necessary to mentally remove yourself from the situation. Like waiting for tea to steep to reach its full potency, you need to let your mind idle in neutral for a while so that it will be at full strength when you move on to the next phase of writing: revision.

Revising your draft. Remember that inner critic—that voice in your head—that you tuned out while you were writing the first draft? It's time to liberate it.

The difference between success and failure in writing rests on the revision process. Sure, it's possible to hand in a first draft, and sometimes you'll even get a passable grade. But if you want to reach your own potential as a writer, you *must* revise.

Following several basic rules can make the revision process work smoothly for you:
- **Read the first draft out loud.** Read your paper out loud—to yourself, a friend, or your computer. It doesn't matter who's listening, as long as you read the first draft out loud.

Reading out loud does several things. You'll more easily discover missing words, verbs that don't match the subject of the sentence, shifts in tense, missing transitions, and other things that you might have to fix. The combination of speaking and reading helps make problems more apparent than if you were simply reading the first draft to yourself silently.

But reading aloud does something more: It slows you down. Speaking takes longer than silent reading, and the slowed pace or oral reading should help you identify things that need revising that you'd otherwise miss.

- **Take the long view.** Start off by taking the broadest perspective possible and asking yourself a series of questions:
  - ❏ Does the paper fulfill its purpose?
  - ❏ Does the paper address every aspect of the assignment for which it was written?
  - ❏ Does the paper respond to what its audience needs to know?
  - ❏ Is the logic of the paper clear to the reader?
  - ❏ Are the transitions between sections clear?
- **Less is more.** Once we've put words on paper, they tend to take on a life of their own—a life which we have created. It is natural to feel a bit parental toward them. However, we need to work against the natural instinct that bids us to nurture and coddle what we've created. Unlike the parents of real children, we need to be merciless and unforgiving with passages, paragraphs, phrases, and words that don't ultimately add to the arguments we're trying to make. Regardless of how fond we may be of our creation, we must cut into it without sympathy.
- **Check sequence and logic.** It's now time to reverse course. Whereas before the focus was on cutting extraneous material, you now need to check what's left with a view toward *adding* material.

  For example, because of earlier deletions, it may be necessary to add or modify transitions between sections and paragraphs. Ideas should flow logically, and the reader should be able to understand the structure in which they are set.
- **Check punctuation and spelling**. Make sure that you've fulfilled the basic requirements of punctuation that have been drummed into you since elementary school. Use a style manual if you're unsure.

  Check spelling carefully. This is one of the areas in which word processors earn their keep: Run the spell-check feature; usually it will not only identify every misspelled word (that is, every word not in its dictionary), but it will prompt you with alternatives for those words that are misspelled.

  Be careful not to rely completely on the spell-checker, however. Such programs can find only misspellings that do not happen to form actual words; if what you typed forms words, the spell-checker will leave it alone, even if the words you typed are not the ones you wanted to use. Foe instants, know spelt-cheek pogrom wood fined eras inn thus settings. And yet every word in it is incorrectly spelled for its purpose.
- **Make it pretty.** Instructors are human. They can't help but react differently to a paper that is neatly typed, compared to one that is handwritten in a difficult-to-read scrawl.

  Take the time, then, to make sure your paper looks good. This doesn't mean that you need to invest in a fancy plastic cover, or worry about the alignment of the staples, or spend a lot of time deciding which font to use on your word processor. But it does mean that the overall impression your paper makes is important, and you should make sure the quality of the paper's appearance matches the quality of the writing.

Evaluate: Acting as Your Own Best Critic

Because you've already put so much work into your paper, you might be tempted to rush through the final stages of the P.O.W.E.R. process. Avoid the temptation. If you've carefully revised your paper, the last stages will not be time-consuming, and they may have a significant impact on your paper's ultimate quality—and your success.

Take these steps to *evaluate* what you've written:

- **Ask yourself if your paper accomplishes what you set out to do.** The beginning of your paper contains a thesis statement and the argument that you intended to make. Does your paper support the thesis? Are the arguments upheld by the evidence you've reported? Would an impartial reader be convinced by what you've written?
- **Put yourself in your instructor's shoes.** Does the paper precisely fit the assignment requirements? Does it meet the instructor's underlying goals in making the assignment?
- **Check the mechanical aspects of the paper.** Make certain the paper represents you the way you want to be represented. Not only should the grammar and spelling be correct, but the paper should look good. If your instructor requires that citations or references be reported in a certain style, make sure you've followed that style.

If you've revised the paper with care, it will likely pass muster. If it doesn't, though, go back and work on it once again. By this point, it should require only minor tinkering to get it into shape.

Rethink: The 3Ms of Writing

Rethinking is the homestretch of the writing process. It's a moment to savor, because it permits you take a long view of what you've accomplished. And it is an accomplishment: You've gone from a blank page to words on paper that tell a story, a story that you've put together. You've turned nothing into something—an achievement in and of itself.

Rethinking occurs on three levels, and you should consider each separately. Think of them as the 3Ms: message, mechanics, and method.

But don't address them until a little time has passed since you completed the evaluation of the paper. Wait a day or so, and then reread the paper. Then reflect on each of the 3Ms:

Rethink the message. Be sure that the overall message your paper conveys is appropriate. A paper is like an advertisement. In most papers, you are seeking to communicate information in order to convince someone of a particular opinion. Make sure that the message is what you wish to communicate, and that ultimately the paper is successful in making the case.

Rethink the mechanics. A television commercial filled with fuzzy images and jerky camera shots would not be very compelling, no matter how good the underlying product. In the same way, a paper with mechanical errors will not impress your readers or persuade them that your arguments are correct. Rethink your writing style, then, to make sure you are putting your best foot forward. Look at grammar, punctuation, and word usage to make sure that the choices you've made are appropriate.

Rethink the method. Every time you finish a paper, you learn something—something about the topic of your writing, and something about yourself. Ask yourself what you have learned to help you become a better writer in the future. What might you have done to improve the writing process? What could have gone better? What will you do differently the next time you write? Finally, reflect on how your writing might have improved as a result of working on this paper.

Above all, remember what you've accomplished: You've transformed what's inside your head—your thoughts, your ideas, your values—into a form that can touch other people. Through your writing, you have exercised the ability to move others, to make them think in new ways, to change them. You've made a difference. That's the real power of writing.

Speaking Your Mind

If you ask first-year college students how much ability they have in various academic endeavors, guess what they generally put at the bottom of their list?[2] Public speaking.

First-year students are not alone. Most people become positively tongue-tied at the mere thought of speaking in front of others. It's not surprising. How often are we so totally exposed, so vulnerable, so open to others' scrutiny? Not only do we have to worry about the message we're communicating—just as with our writing—but in addition each of us has to be concerned about nonverbal behavior and the impression we're conveying. Am I slouching? Is my clothing in disarray? Am I sweating so much it's noticeable? Do I have a silly expression on my face?

In My Own Words
How I Feel about Public Speaking

Just how do you feel about speaking in public? Explore your feelings—and see if there's any part of the experience that you feel good about—by considering these questions.

What was the worst experience you ever had with public speaking? Why was it so bad?

Was it worse before, during, or after speaking? How did you manage to get through it?

Had you spent time preparing what you were going to say? Were you well organized?

After you spoke, did you feel you had done well or poorly? Why?

What did your audience say about your speaking? How do you think they felt while you were speaking? Were they wishing you'd fail or succeed?

Do you think other people feel better about speaking in public than you do? Does anyone you know actually like it?

Ask a few of your friends how they feel about public speaking, and note their responses here:

What was the best experience you ever had with public speaking? What made this experience bearable?

What's the difference between your worst experience and your best one? What factors were different?

Although it's unlikely that you'll fully rid yourself of your fears about speaking, it's important to keep several points in mind:

- **Audiences are generally sympathetic.** They've all been where you are and probably share your fears about public speaking. They're on your side and are rooting for you to succeed.
- **Once you start speaking, it will become easier.** Anxiety tends to be highest *before* you start talking. Most people find that after they start a talk, their nervousness tends to decline.
- **Practice, practice, practice.** The secret to successful public speaking is that there is no secret. The primary rule is that success rests on practice. The more you practice and prepare for the talk, the better you'll do. It's that simple.

Keep in mind, too, that in many fundamental ways, speaking is like writing. You need to consider who your audience is, muster your arguments, and decide how to sequence those arguments. Consequently, the P.O.W.E.R. writing framework that we presented earlier in the chapter largely applies to speaking as well:

- **Prepare** what you will say and how you will say it. Think about your audience and the occasion on which you will speak, and try to be sure your words match both audience and occasion.
- **Organize** your thoughts, using notes to cue you to the main parts of your presentation and making logical connections for your audience to follow.
- **Work** carefully during your presentation by speaking clearly and calmly to your audience and avoiding distracting mannerisms or body language.
- **Evaluate** your performance after you finish your presentation and ask others to evaluate it, too. Take notes on the feedback you receive from yourself and others.
- **Rethink** your entire approach to preparing for and delivering presentations each time you make one. Make the changes you feel you should make to improve your performance over time.

The uniqueness of speech. Although speaking and writing, which are both concerned with communicating your thoughts to others, share many features, they are not exactly the same. In fact, speaking presents several unique challenges. Among the factors that you need to take into account when you are speaking are these:

- **The first minute counts—a lot.** It's make-or-break in the first minute of any talk. If you can get your audience's attention, arouse their interest, and engage them in the first few minutes, you're on your way to a successful speech. On the other hand, let them drift off early on, and you've lost them, potentially for good.

  How do you get them interested? There are several ways:
  - ❑ **Begin with an anecdote.** ("It was a scientist's dream, experienced as he dozed off in front of a fire, that led to one of the most important biological discoveries of all time.")
  - ❑ **Start with a quotation.** (" 'I have seen the enemy, and he is us.' But are we really the enemy? I believe…")
  - ❑ **Arouse their curiosity.** ("I have a secret, one that I've kept hidden for many years—until now.")
  - ❑ **Talk about the significance of the topic.** ("If you think that spousal abuse is not a problem, take a look at the prevalence of abuse in American households.")
  - ❑ Ask a question. ("Have you ever wondered how you could improve your self-esteem?")
  - ❑ **Use humor.** ("I'm going to talk a bit today about paranoia. Why are you looking at me that way? Is there something on my face?")
- **Provide oral transition points.** When we're reading a textbook selection, we usually have the luxury of knowing exactly when a transition point occurs. It's marked by a title, section

heading, or new paragraph. These markers help us construct a mental map that permits us to understand the overall structure of the piece we're reading.

Listeners don't have the same advantage. Unless the speaker orally signals that they are moving to a new part of a talk, they'll get lost. Not only will they be unable to understand the structure of the talk, they won't know where the talk is headed.

However, there are several ways to erect verbal signposts throughout a speech. By using phrases such as the following, you can alert listeners that a twist in the journey lies ahead:

- ❑ "To understand the problem, we need to consider…"
- ❑ "The problems are clearly daunting. But there are solutions. Let's consider some of them…"
- ❑ "Now that we've considered the solutions, we need to take a look at their costs…"
- ❑ "Let's go back for a moment to an earlier point I made…"
- ❑ "To sum up, the situation offers some unexpected advantages…"

- **Use notes effectively.** Develop an outline that includes the major points you wish to cover, and have this outline in front of you when you speak. It might be written or typed on a sheet of paper, or you might use 3" x 5" or 4" x 6" notecards. (Number them!) In addition, write out and memorize your opening and closing statements.

  By memorizing the opening and closing statements, you'll have the opportunity to look your audience in the eye and engage them nonverbally at two of the most crucial junctures in your talk—the beginning and the end. Using an outline for most of your talk permits you to sound natural as you speak. You'll probably use slightly different words every time you give your talk, which is fine.

- **Use visual aids: Seeing is believing**. Maps, photos, drawings, figures, and other illustrations add another dimension to a presentation, helping to engage listeners. You can even use props. For example, if you are talking about the impact of psychological principles on the legal system, you might incorporate a gavel into your talk. Visual aids make abstract concepts more concrete and immediate.

  Visual aids serve another function: They can reduce your anxiety. You can be assured that when an audience is focusing on an illustration or prop, their attention is drawn away from you, at least temporarily. Just knowing this may be enough to lower your anxiety level.

- **Use the right amount and kind of practice**. Although running through your speech mentally will help you to familiarize yourself with your presentation, it's not as effective as actually giving the speech aloud. It is only by hearing yourself speak that you can actually get a sense of how well you're coming across.

  You should also practice in front of a friend or classmate. It is only by actually trying your talk out in front of a warm body that you'll be able to approximate the experience of actually speaking in public. In addition, an audience can provide you with feedback regarding what is working and what points need clarification.

  How much practice is enough practice? You've probably done enough when you do a good job giving a talk twice in a row. That's sufficient; you don't want to overpractice. If you practice your talk too many times, you'll become so bored with it that the actual talk will sound canned and unconvincing.

- **Fight stage fright.** Although you won't be able to alleviate your stage fright completely, several techniques can reduce the anxiety that public speaking produces. First, make sure you're wearing clothes that are comfortable and that make you look good on the day of a talk. If you feel good about your appearance, you'll be more relaxed.

  Five minutes before you get up to speak, take three slow, deep breaths. Concentrate on the feeling of the air going in and out of your body. If a particular part of your body feels tense, tighten it up even more and then relax this. Do it several times. Finally, visualize yourself giving the speech successfully and the relief that you'll feel afterwards.

- **Monitor your nonverbal behavior**. To avoid appearing as if you were scared to death—even if you are—stand up straight and tall. Let your hands fall comfortably at your sides, using them smoothly—not jerkily—when you need to gesture to make a point. Look directly at different members of your audience, shifting your gaze from one person to the next. Eye contact engages audience members, making them feel that your words are directed straight toward them.

   If the thought of eye contact scares you, try a trick that some speakers use. Look directly at the *hairline* of different audience members; to your listeners, this is generally indistinguishable from eye contact, and yet it can help you avoid becoming distracted by a facial expression that you may interpret—or misinterpret—negatively: "Is she bored?" "Is he angry at what I'm saying?"

Speaking Off-the-cuff: Extemporaneous Speaking

If there is one thing that is even more anxiety-producing than giving a prepared talk, it's public speaking that is extemporaneous. **Extemporaneous talks** are unprepared, off-the-cuff presentations.

Ironically, though, extemporaneous speaking happens far more frequently than you may at first think. Consider, for example, what you have to do when an instructor calls on you in class and asks, "What do you think the point of this article was?" The response you give is very much an exercise in extemporaneous speaking. Or how about when you visit your landlord to complain about the water heater that keeps breaking, and the landlord asks you for details about the problem. In fact, in one sense, every time you hold a conversation you're engaging in extemporaneous speaking.

Try It! #2
Put Yourself on the Spot—Pretest

Have a classmate write five controversial questions (e.g., "Should abortion be legalized?") on separate notecards. Place the cards, face down, on a table in front of you. Choose one of the cards at random, and immediately answer the question as well as you can. Repeat the test using a second card. Leave the three remaining cards on the table for the next *Try It!* exercise—the posttest.

"Prepping" to speak extemporaneously. Because extemporaneous speaking is, by definition, unplanned, it is hard to prepare for it in advance. Still, there is a simple process that you can use when you're put on the spot. Known as the PREP formula,[3] it consists of breaking down an answer into four parts:

- **Point of view.** Initially provide your point of view, delineating a clear view of where you stand on the issue.
- **Reasons.** Provide the chief reasons why you believe your position is correct.
- **Evidence or examples.** Give specific evidence to support your point of view.
- **Point of view, restated.** Restate your point of view.

Here's an example:

Professor Fiske: Who can tell me if racism is a uniquely American problem? Stephanie, why don't you take a stab at the question.

Stephanie: I don't believe racism is uniquely American at all **[point of view].** If we look at other times in history or other parts of the world today, we find all sorts of racial problems **[reasons].** For example, consider Bosnia and the Middle East.

Or look at the difficulties that South Africa is having. Or look at Nazi Germany **[evidence or examples].** So it's hard for me to understand how anyone could contend that racism is uniquely American. Racism, unfortunately, is a universal fact of life **[point of view, restated].**

Although using the PREP system initially will be difficult, you'll find it easy to learn. And with sufficient practice, it will become automatic.

Try It! #3
Put Yourself on the Spot—Posttest

Return to the three cards remaining on the table after the last *Try It!* exercise. Choose one of the cards at random, and immediately answer the question—this time using the PREP system. Do the same with the remaining cards. Then answer the following questions:

Did you notice a difference in your answers to these three questions, compared with your answers to the two questions you addressed without the PREP system?

What differences did you find? Did they system affect the quantity (i.e., length) of your answers? The quality of your answers?

When you used the PREP system, did you notice a difference in your third answer, compared with your first? Did you get better at using the system?

Can you think of any modifications in PREP that might make it work better for you?

WEB P.O.W.E.R.

Grammar and Style
1) http://www.english.upenn/~jlynch/Grammar/
This site provides a miscellaneous list of grammatical rules and explanations, comments on style, and suggestions on usage. There are two types of entries: specific articles on usage, and more general articles on style. An alphabetical search engine is provided to help locate information more quickly.

2) http://www.cc.columbia.edu/acis/bartleby/strunk/index.html
Based on the classic text recommended by writing instructors for many years, Strunk's *The Elements of Style*, this site is filled with helpful hints on word usage, punctuation, and common mistakes to avoid. This site is a must for writers serious about improving their writing.

Research Papers

3) http://webster.comnet.edu/mla.htm

The site describes the stages involved in writing a research paper including how to gather research information; creating outlines; avoiding plagiarism, and formatting a paper. The site can take you through the paper writing process step-by-step.

Speeches

4) http://www.la.psu.edu/speech/100a/workbook/wrkbk.htm

This site is an online tutorial for preparing an effective speech. The tutorial takes you through the step-by-step process of preparing a speech, including selecting an appropriate topic, analyzing one's audience, and structuring a speech.

Sources for Experimental Research Papers

http://www.southwestern.edu/~giuliant/apastyle.html
A hypertext guide to writing experimental research reports for psychology students.

Publication Manual of the American Psychological Association (4th ed.). (1994). Washington, D.C.: American Psychological Association.

---

[1] Elbow, Peter. (1998) *Writing With Power.* 2nd ed. NY: Oxford University Press.
[2] Higher Education Research Institute, UCLA, Annual Survey.
[3] Wydro, K. *Thinking on Your Feet: The Art of Thinking and Speaking under Pressure.* Englewood Cliffs, NJ: Prentice Hall.

Chapter 4

P.O.W.E.R. Memory

Acetylcholine...norepinephrine...gamma aminobutyric acid...Jasmine Morenita didn't know how she was ever going to remember all the different neurotransmitters and what they did. Jasmine had a good memory for some things; she could call to mind a vivid picture of any of the hundreds of movies she'd seen over the last couple of years, but she had trouble remembering the names of new people she'd met last week at her friend Lucy's party.

She had chosen psychology as her major because she was really interested in why people behave as they do. Physiological Psychology was exciting because it addressed how people's own bodies influenced their behavior, but how was she ever going to remember all of these complicated terms? She'd never been good at rote memorization. There had to be some way she could make the memory skills she did have work for her.

Looking Ahead

Many of us complain about our memories. We never think they're good enough. Yet each of us has memories that express the scope of human emotions, as well as holding our intellectual backgrounds. Our memories permit us to know that $2 + 2 = 4$, how to change the oil in our car, and the date of our birth. They let us recall who Sigmund Freud is, the speed of light, and the way to figure out the area of a triangle. Memory represents the story of our lives, a book on whose pages our past existence is spelled out.

In this chapter, we'll consider the role that memory plays in bringing us success in psychology. We'll examine why memory fails and take a close look at ways to improve memory and learn information in a way that will help us recall it when we need it.

You Must Remember This

There's one well-kept secret about memory, and you should never forget it: You remember everything.

Sure, sometimes you have trouble recalling information that you know you've learned. Or maybe you don't recall that you learned it, even though in fact you did. But this is not because information has disappeared from your head. The problem is one of *retrieval*. **Retrieval** entails finding information stored in memory and returning it to consciousness for further use. Every piece of information that we've ever learned is buried somewhere in the brain. The problem is that we can't always find it.

The proof of this assertion comes from a growing understanding of the physiology of memory. Consider what happens when you're exposed to some new material. Let's say your geometry instructor spends a class talking about the Pythagorean formula in geometry, which says that the square of the length of the hypotenuse of a right triangle is equal to the sum of the squares of the two other sides. (You may well recall this formula as $a^2 + b^2 = c^2$.)

At the moment you learn the formula, the wiring connecting a handful of the seventy trillion or so brain cells in your head is changed—forever. The information on the Pythagorean formula is etched into some tiny part of your brain, and unless that part of the brain is damaged in some way through injury or disease, it will stay there for the remainder of your life. This doesn't mean that you will easily find the information when you need it. But it does mean that that particular piece of information remains patiently in place, potentially retrievable the next time you encounter a geometry problem.

The practical outgrowth of this biological process is straightforward: You already remember everything you need to know, and a lot more. With some effort, you could remember the names of everyone in your third-grade class. You know what you ate when you went to the eighth-grade dance. You remember the name of the body of water that borders Iraq. And you even could have remembered where you left your keys the last time you misplaced them.

It also means that your memory is every bit as good as that of the memory experts you sometimes see on television. You could, for example, memorize ten pages of the New York City telephone book—every name, address, and phone number—and recall them flawlessly—if you wanted to.

The key to successful recall is to learn the material initially in a way that will allow us to recall it easily later. And if we have trouble remembering material that we've already learned, we must figure out a way to retrieve it from our memory bank. In short, we need to devise ways to set loose the memories that reside within. We need to unleash the memories that are just waiting to be emancipated.

Try It! #1
Remembering the Details

Read the following story. Pay attention to the details, but don't take notes or make lists.

Demain entered the marketplace slowly, feeling his way. He had never seen such confusion.

Hundreds of wagons, caravans, booths, and carts were drawn up in a broad U, occupying three sides of the enormous town square, their awnings and curtains open and inviting. The colors and odors were a sensual assault; he perceived them not just through his eyes and nose, but as if they were pressing forcibly against his skin. And the sounds! He could scarcely keep himself from bolting back they way he had come, to the safety of the countryside.

A sense of wonder pushed him forward. He walked past gold merchants, with their gray cloaks and watchful eyes, and a potter, her shop filled three shelves high with vases, bottles, and jars of deep blues, reds, and yellows that Demain—accustomed to the brown clay that adorned his mother's kitchen—had never even imagined possible. Cloths were on sale in the booth next to the potter's—shamelessly long bolts of impossibly patterned prints, depicting herons, bulls, schools of fish, a field of wheat, great bowls of fruit, and men and women engaged in the pursuits he knew from stories: They danced in bold colors and graceful postures, harvested vast fields of bounty, fought battles of intricate strategy, and drank and courted in riotous taverns.

Past the dealers in rugs, chairs, hats, shoes, and wagons; past the blacksmith's huge muddy arms beating out rugged tools and fine weapons; past the fortune tellers and musicians, Demain at last came to the vendors of food and drink. Never had he felt so hungry. He was lifted off his feet—he swore he was floating—by the aroma of long lines of sausages, sides of beef, whole lambs, chickens on spits the length of spears, bacon and hams, fried potatoes, great vats of boiling vegetables, stewing tomatoes, and breads—all shapes and sizes of loaves, twisted into braids, curled into circles, flattened, puffed, elongated, pocketed, and glazed.

Demain felt the two coppers in his pocket—his holiday bounty—and hoped they would be enough.

We'll come back to the story of Demain later in this chapter, but before proceeding, take a trip down your own memory lane. Contemplate the role that memory plays in your own life by completing the "In My Own Words" section.

In My Own Words
What Sort of Memory Do I Have?

What is the very first thing you remember in your life?

Are you best at remembering faces, shapes, colors, smells, names, dates, or facts?

What did your kitchen smell like when you were growing up? What did your elementary school smell like? Do you think you could tell them apart if you were led into one of them blindfolded?

What color is the cover of this book? What color clothes was your psychology professor wearing the last time you were in class?

Do you ever find yourself recognizing someone's face but being unable to recall the name that goes with it? What do you do? When you're introduced to new people, do you do anything special to remember their names?

Are you good at trivia contests? Can you recall factual information quickly, such as the capital of Alaska, the name of the sixth president, last year's Best Picture, Best Actor, and Best Actress?

Are you good at remembering important personal dates, such as birthdays? How about dates of historical events? Phone numbers?

Do you ever feel that information is "on the tip of your tongue" but you just can't seem to get it out? Have you ever recalled the information you were seeking just a few minutes too late?

How are you at remembering lists, such as a list of things to buy at a store?

Would you like to have a better memory? Have you ever tried to improve your memory?

Prepare: Remembering the Right Stuff

Memorize what you need to memorize. Forget about the rest.

The average textbook chapter has something like 20,000 words. If you had to recall every word of the chapter, it would be nearly impossible. Furthermore, it would be counterproductive, a waste of time. Sheer memorization might permit you to spew out definitions of key terms or to identify dates, but it has little to do with the more important ability to recall and deeply understand psychological material in meaningful ways.

But let's look at the material in a psychology chapter in a different way. Lurking within those 20,000 words might be only 20 different concepts. And perhaps there are only 10 key words that are totally unfamiliar to you. *Those* are the pieces of information that should be the focus of your efforts to memorize.

In short, the first step in building a better memory is to determine just what it is that you wish to recall. By extracting what is important from what is less crucial, you'll be able to limit the amount and extent of the material that you need to recall and focus, laser-like, on what you need to remember.

To be able to determine what is important, look at the overall, big picture. Don't get lost in minute details. Instead, prepare yourself by taking a broad overview of the material you need to know, and decide what your goal is going to be.

Organize: Arranging for Memory

Don't think of memorization as pumping gasoline (new information) into an almost-empty gas tank (your brain). You're not filling something that is empty. On the contrary, you are filling a container that already has a lot of things in it, that is infinitely expandable, and that never empties out.

Try It! #2
Getting Your Memory Organized

As critical thinking expert Diane Halpern points out, having an organized memory is like having a neat bedroom: Its value is that you know you'll be able to find something when you need it. To prove the point, try this exercise she devised.[1]

Before beginning the exercise, cover the bottom half of this page. Now read the following 15 words at a rate of approximately one per second:

> girl
> heart
> robin
> purple
> finger
> flute
> blue
> organ
> man
> hawk
> green
> lung
> eagle
> child
> piano

Cover the list and write down as many of the words as you can.
How many words were you able to list?

Now read the following list:

green
blue
purple
man
girl
child
piano
flute
organ
heart
lung
finger
eagle
hawk
robin

Now cover this list and write down as many words as you can remember.

How many words did you remember this time?

You probably noticed that the words in both lists are identical, but it's likely that you remembered more of them the second time through. Some of the improvement is due to your increased familiarity with the words the second time you read them, because you had seen them before. But most of the improvement comes from the fact that the second list organizes the words according to their meaning, as groups of colors, people, musical instruments, body parts, and birds. They were easier to remember because they were *meaningfully* organized, instead of being random.

This simple demonstration illustrates an important point with profound implications: You can improve your ability to remember information by organizing it effectively. When you study, look at the interconnections between the various parts of the material, and group different bits of information according to categories. You will then have a structure in your memory to which the individual pieces belong. Remembering one piece of information from a category on that structure will help you remember the others. Even if your bedroom can't be neat and tidy, your memory can be!

In order to optimize memorization, then, you need to organize and consolidate new information with your existing memories. That means thinking about new information within the context of what you already know. If you approach each new memorization task as something entirely new and unrelated to your previous knowledge, you'll have enormous difficulty recalling it. On the other hand, if you integrate it with what you already know, you'll be able to learn it more easily and recall it far better than if you just dump it into your head.

Obviously, you're not going to be able to reach inside your head, find the right spot, and carve out a place for the new information that you're trying to add. But you can make your brain do the organizational work for you by thinking about the associations the new material has with the old.

Another aspect of organization is the association between memory and place. *Where* you learn something makes a difference in how well you can recall it. Memory researchers have found that people actually remember things better in the place where they first studied and learned them. Consequently, one of the ways to jog your memory is to try to recreate the situation in which you first learned what you're trying to remember. If you memorized Maslow's hierarchy of needs while you were lying in bed, it might be helpful during a test to recall correct order of the needs by thinking about—"recreating"—your previous study session in bed.

Another effective place-related strategy is to introduce new data into your mind in the place that you know you're going to need to recall it at some future moment. For instance, suppose you know that you're going to be tested on certain material in the room in which your class is held. Try to do at least some of your studying in that same room. Then, when you take the test, the associations you've formed between the material and the physical location of your studying may aid your recall.

Work: Memory Tricks of the Trade

One of the good things about the work of memorization is that you have your choice of literally dozens of techniques. Depending on the kind of material you need to recall and your prior exposure to related information, you can turn to any number of procedures.

As we sort through the various options, keep in mind that very often the choice is yours. Use what works for you, and discard the others. No one strategy works for everyone, and you should empower yourself to reject those that just don't seem effective for you. At the same time, you should feel free to add to the list strategies that have worked for you in the past.

Mnemonics: Priming Memory

Mnemonics. This odd word (pronounced in an equally odd fashion, with the "m" silent—"neh MON ix") describes formal organization techniques used to make material more readily remembered. Mnemonic techniques are in fact the tricks-of-the-trade that professional memory experts use, and you too can use them to recall lists of items of the sort that you will often need to recall for tests.

- **Acronyms.**

  - ❑ FACE
  - ❑ Roy G. Biv
  - ❑ P.O.W.E.R. Learning

  You're already well acquainted with **acronyms,** words or phrases formed by the first letters of a series of terms. For instance, FACE spells out the names of the notes that appear in the spaces on the G Clef music staff ("F," "A," "C," and "E," starting at the bottom of the staff.) Roy G. Biv is a favorite of psychology students studying perception who must remember the colors of the spectrum (**r**ed, **o**range, **y**ellow, **g**reen, **b**lue, **i**ndigo, and **v**iolet). And P.O.W.E.R. stands for—well, you probably remember by this point in the book.

  The benefit of acronyms is that they help us to recall a complete list of steps or items. The drawback, though, is that the acronym itself has to be remembered, and sometimes we may not recall it when we need it. For instance, Roy G. Biv is not exactly the sort of name that readily comes to mind. And if we're unable to remember an acronym, it won't be of much use to us. Even if we do remember Roy G. Biv, we might get stuck trying to recall what a particular letter stands for. (For example, we'd probably prefer not to spend a lot of time during a test trying to remember if the "B" stands for brown, or beige, or blue.)

- **Acrostics.** After learning to use the acronym "FACE" to remember the notes on the spaces of the music staff, many beginning musicians learn that the names of the lines on the staff form the acrostic, "**E**very **G**ood **B**oy **D**eserves **F**udge." **Acrostics** are sentences in which the first letters spell out something that needs to be recalled. The benefits—as well as the drawbacks—of acrostics are similar to those of acronyms.

- **Rhymes and jingles**. "Thirty days hath September, April, June, and November…" If you know the rest of the rhyme, you're familiar with one of the most commonly used mnemonic jingles in the English language. Similarly, some of us learned the main theme of Schubert's Unfinished Symphony by singing the words, "This is the symphony that Schubert wrote and never finished" when the theme first appears. For those who learned to recognize the symphony by using this mnemonic, it is virtually impossible to hear the symphony without recalling the words.

Although mnemonics are helpful, keep in mind that they have a number of significant shortcomings. First, they don't focus on the meaning of the items being remembered. Instead, mnemonic devices use characteristics such as the letters that make up the words being memorized. Consequently, the information is learned by rote, rather than considering what it means and thinking critically about its relationship to other material. Because information that is learned in terms of its surface characteristics— such as first letters that form a word—is less likely to be retained than information that is learned in terms of its meaning, mnemonic devices are an imperfect route to memorization.

There's another problem with mnemonics: Sometimes it takes as much effort to create a mnemonic device as it would to memorize the material in the first place. And because the mnemonic itself has no meaning, it can be forgotten.

Despite their drawbacks, the use of mnemonics can be profitable. They are particularly helpful when the material being memorized is composed of a list of items or a series of steps.

The Method of Loci

The ancient Greeks had a way with words. Their orators could deliver long speeches, some of which went on for hours, with nary a note in front of them. How did they remember what they wanted to say?

They used a procedure called the **method of loci.** "Loci" is the Latin word for "places," and it helps describe a procedure in which each part of a speech is thought of as "residing" in a different place in a building.

Consider, for example, a speech that has three major sections: an introduction, a main body, and a conclusion. Imagine further that each of the three sections has various subcomponents that you need to recall.

To use the method of loci, you'd first visualize the living room, kitchen, and bedroom of a house with which you were familiar. Next, you'd mentally "place" the introduction of the speech into the living room of the house. Each of the parts of the introduction would be "dropped" on a different piece of furniture, according to how the furniture was laid out in the room (e.g., proceeding clockwise from the door). The easy chair might contain the first point of the introduction, the sofa the next point, and an end table the last point. Then you'd move into the kitchen and do the same thing with the body of the paper, laying out your arguments on different pieces of furniture. Finally, you'd end up in the bedroom, where you'd "place" the conclusion.

The technique is a powerful one, and it can be adapted to a variety of memory tasks. For instance, to learn a list of words, you could place each one in a series of sequential locations in a room. For instance, to recall your grocery list you might think up a set of outlandish, striking images: peanut butter spread across the entryway carpet, a stalk of celery in a vase, Wheaties strewn like rose petals across the couch, and a geyser of milk emanating from the top of the lamp. Later, at the grocery store, a mental stroll through the living room would help you recall the items you needed to buy.

Try It! #3
Room with a View: The Method of Loci

This is a chance to try out the method of loci. Picture as clearly as you can a room with which you are very familiar. Mentally stand in the entry to the room and place the items on the following list, one by one, on the furniture inside the room, starting from your left and continuing clockwise around the room. Try to make the images you form as outrageous as possible.

1. diet cola
2. hot dogs
3. bread
4. salted crackers
5. tuna fish
6. macaroni and cheese
7. bottled water
8. milk
9. lettuce
10. tomatoes
11. rice
12. orange juice
13. aspirin
14. coat hangers
15. trash bags

How did you do? Write down your score here:

You will get even better at this method if you decide to keep using it. Try it one more time with a more challenging list:

1. Eddie Murphy
2. Sigourney Weaver
3. Mel Gibson
4. Oprah Winfrey
5. Jackie Chan
6. Michelle Pfeiffer
7. Denzel Washington
8. Winona Ryder
9. Charlie Sheen
10. Vanessa Williams
11. John Leguizamo
12. Uma Thurman
13. Kevin Bacon
14. Meg Ryan
15. Sean Connery

How many did you get right this time?

The Peg Method

A close cousin of the method of loci, the **peg method** uses a series of key words tied to numbers to help in the recall of numeric information. For instance, a set of "pegs" that you could use would link numbers with these words:

One is a sun,
Two is a zoo,
Three is me,
Four is a store,
Five is a dive,
Six are sticks,
Seven is heaven,
Eight is a gate,
Nine is a pine,
Ten is a den.

By thinking of exotic images using the peg words tied to the numbers, you can recall specific numbers that you need to memorize. For instance, suppose you had trouble remembering the value of *pi*, used to calculate the circumference of a circle (3.14, in case you don't remember). Translate the number into the relevant peg words—me (three), sun (one), and store (four)—and imagine an image linking the three. One obvious possibility is an image of yourself wearing sunglasses, heading out to a store on a sunny day. A less obvious and more exotic possibility is an image of yourself bowling a large sun into the front of a store.

The peg system can also be used to memorize ordered lists of items, when the sequence in which they appear is important. In this use, the peg system is very similar to the method of loci. You simply link images of the ordered set of items to the ten "numbers." The first item is linked with the sun, the second with a zoo, and so on.

Try It! #4
Pegging the Memory

After you've learned the "peg" poem, you'll be surprised how easy it is to use. Try it. Use the peg system to memorize the words on the list below, in numerical order. For instance, for the first word, think of an image that links a cactus with the sun (remember: "one is the sun" from the poem). Do the same for the rest of the words on the list.

1. cactus
2. book
3. globe
4. soda
5. pencil
6. fork
7. gun
8. ruler
9. cigarette
10. car

Now cover up the list.
What number is the ruler? What is number four on the list? You'll probably be surprised as to how easy it is.

<u>Involve Multiple Senses</u>

The more senses you can involve when you're trying to learn new material, the better you'll be able to remember. Here's why: Every time we encounter new information, all of our senses are potentially at work. For instance, if we witness a car crash, we receive sensory input from the sight of the two cars hitting each other, the sound of the impact, and perhaps the smell of burning rubber. Each piece of sensory information is stored in a separate location in the brain, and yet all the pieces are linked together in extraordinarily intricate ways.

What this means is that when we seek to remember the details of the crash, recalling a memory of one of the sensory experiences—such as what we heard—can trigger memories of the other types of memories. For example, thinking about the *sound* the two cars made when they hit can bring back memories of the way the scene *looked*.

You can make use of the fact that memories are stored in multiple ways by applying the following techniques:

- **When you learn something, use your body.** Don't sit passively at your desk. Instead, move around. Stand up; sit down. Touch the page. Trace figures with your fingers. Talk to yourself. Think out loud.

  Such "strange" behavior increases the number of modalities in which the information is stored. By involving every part of your body, you've increased the number of ways potentially to trigger a relevant memory later, when you need to recall it. And when one memory is triggered, other related memories may come tumbling back.

- **Draw and diagram the material.** We've already considered (in Chapter 2) the power of concept maps, the method of structuring written material by graphically grouping and connecting key ideas and themes. When we create a concept map, one of the things we're doing is expanding the modalities in which information can be stored in our minds.

  Other types of drawing can be useful in aiding later recall. Creating drawings, sketches, and even cartoons can help us remember better. Your creations don't have to be Great Art, or detailed, involved illustrations. Even rough sketches are effective, because creating them gets both the visual and tactile senses involved.

- **Visualize. <u>Visualization</u>** is a technique by which images are formed to ensure that material arrives in long-term memory. Visualization serves several purposes. It helps us in moving from the abstract to the concrete. It engages multiple senses. It permits us to figuratively link different of bits of information together. It provides us with a context for storing information.

  What kind of visualizations work best? There's a simple rule: Weird is good. The more extreme, outlandish, and eccentric the image you create, the easier it will be to remember. And if you can remember the image, you'll probably remember the information that's attached to it.

- **Think positively.** Emotions matter. If we're in a negative frame of mind when we try to memorize something, our negative feelings can become attached to the memory. But the same thing works the other way: If we think positively about the process of memorization, those more positive feelings will end up being etched into our memory.

  Of course our feelings are not so moldable that we can turn them off in the same way we're able to turn off the power at the flip of an electric switch. But just recognizing our feelings can help decrease their power to influence and block memories.

<u>Overlearning</u>

Overlearning consists of studying and rehearsing material past the point of initial mastery. Through overlearning, recall becomes automatic. Rather than searching for a fact, going through mental contortions until perhaps the information surfaces, overlearning permits us to recall the information without even thinking about it.

To put the principle of overlearning to work, don't stop studying at the point when you can say to yourself, "Well, I'll probably pass this test." You may be right, but that's all you'll do—pass. Instead, spend extra time learning the material until it becomes as familiar as an old, comfortable shoe. At that point, overlearning has occurred, and you'll be able to recall the material with ease.

Evaluate: Can You Recall?

All the tricks of the memory trade have brought you to a point where you probably feel comfortable in your ability to remember the material you've been learning. Now it's time to test yourself, to evaluate whether you'll be able to recall the material when you need it. There are several ways to evaluate your memory:

- **Take advantage of in-text review questions and tests.** Many psychology textbook chapters end with a quiz or a set of review questions about the material. Some have questions scattered throughout the chapter. Exploit them! Not only do such questions indicate what the writer of the book thought was important for you to learn and memorize, but they can provide an excellent opportunity for evaluating your memory later.
- **Test yourself.** Temporarily transform yourself into your instructor, and prioritize what you're most likely to be tested on. Then create your own test, writing out some questions.

   Later, after as little as a few hours, take the test, and then grade it. How have you done? If you've achieved a "grade" that you're satisfied with, then fine. If, on the other hand, you've missed some key pieces of information, then you'll want to return to work and spend more time on memorization.
- **Team up with a friend.** When it comes to evaluating your memory, two heads are often better than one. Working with a classmate can help you test the limits of your memory and assess areas in which you need work.

   For instance, you and a friend can take turns testing yourselves, switching back and forth between asking and answering questions. Turn it into a contest: One of you plays Alex Trebek of *Jeopardy,* and the other plays a contestant. You can even work in groups. The important thing is to switch who's asking and who's answering the questions. And keep this in mind: even when you're directing questions to others—officially evaluating their memory—you're simultaneously giving your own memory a workout.

Rethink: Consolidating Memories

Like fine wines, memories need time to age. Psychologists talk about this as the process of "**memory consolidation**." What this means is that the physical links between brain cells that represent memory in the brain need time to become fixed and stable. This process explains why information is not suddenly and permanently established in long-term memory the first time we're exposed to it. In fact, the process of consolidation may continue for days and even—in some cases—for years.[2]

Obviously you don't have years to wait. But it does pay to try to memorize material in advance of the time that you'll really need to use it. Then, when you go back to reconsider it, it will be well established in your mind.

Furthermore, the phenomenon of memory consolidation explains why cramming is not a great idea. Cramming is the process of spending the preceding evening or even the hours just before a test trying to memorize as much as possible. The memories that come from cramming simply don't last. It's far more effective to distribute studying over many shorter sessions, rather than squeezing it into a single, long session just before a test. Fatigue and anxiety prevent long, last-minute practice sessions from being as effective as practice that is spread out.

The best way to ensure good memory is to return to the material even after your personal evaluation tells you that you can recall it easily. Wait several days, if possible, and then review it again. You'll be able to identify the aspects of the material that you know well, as well as the things that just haven't jelled yet in long-term memory. Rethinking the material, then, not only permits you to take another look at the stuff of your memory, but helps you identify where you need more work.

Try It! #5
Remember Demain

Remember the passage earlier in this chapter about Demain, who found himself in the midst of a colorful, aromatic bazaar of booths and shops? Without turning back to the passage, write down everything you can remember about what Demain experienced in the marketplace—the shops, sights, and foods.

Now read the passage, trying to remember its details by using one or more techniques from this chapter. You might use the method of loci, the peg method, the method of organizing ideas into chunks, or other techniques. Then answer these questions about the passage.

1. What scenes were depicted on the cloths?

2. What were the gold merchants wearing?

3. After the cloth shop, what businesses did Demain pass to arrive at the vendors of food and drink?

4. What foods did Demain see and smell at the fair?

WEB P.O.W.E.R.

Concept Mapping

1) http://www.coun.uvic.ca/learn/program/hndouts/map_ho.html

This site aids in concept mapping, an effective memory aid that improves recall and understanding by building meaning structures around key concepts.

Mnemonics

2) http://www.coun.uvic.ca/learn/program/hndouts/mnemon.html

In this site, you'll find some good examples of mnemonics like "On Old Olympus' Towering Tops A Fat Angelic Girl Viewed Spanish Hops" which is a tongue twisting mnemonic for remembering the cranial nerves. (In case you don't have them already memorized, the cranial nerves are Olfactory, Optic, Oculomotor, Trochlear, Trigeminal, Abducent, Facial, Auditory, Glossopharyngeal, Vagar, Spinal Accessory, Hypoglossal).

Memory Techniques

3) http://www.mindtools.com/memory.html

This site provides access to several methods for significantly improving the power of your memory. The process of memory itself is described and several memory techniques are explained. Examples of how each memory technique can be applied to such topics as remembering lists and learning foreign languages are also included.

---

[1] Halpern, D.F., 1996. *Thought and Knowledge: An Introduction to Critical Thinking.* Mahwah, NJ: Erlbaum, 48.
[2] Abel et al., 1995; Squire.

Chapter 5

Time Management

It was the first week of college and Mark Josephs could not believe how great it was..."It's amazing! No parents on your back all the time telling you what to do. No teachers assigning homework every night to make sure you do your reading. I get to choose my own schedule so I don't take any Friday classes. This is definitely the life."

Six weeks later things are not so great for Mark..."I have an Intro Psych paper topic and a Calculus homework due at the end of this week. I have exams in French and Intro Psych next week. I have so much reading to do that I don't even know where to start. What happened? I've been having such a good time. I've been going to my classes—well, mostly. I meet friends at the library a couple of times a week. How could I have gotten so behind? When am I going to get caught up?"

Looking Ahead

Have you had a semester like Mark's? Does time just seem to slip away from you? Are you constantly trying to cram more activities into less time? Do you feel as if you never have enough time?

You're not alone: Most people wish they had more time to accomplish the things they need to do. However, some people are a lot better at juggling their time than others. What's their secret?

There is no secret. No one has more than 168 hours a week, no matter how industrious they may be. Instead, it comes down to figuring out our priorities and managing our time better.

In this chapter we examine strategies for improving our time management skills. We begin by discussing the importance of controlling time, and we look at a way to account for the ways we currently use—and misuse—time. We explore some strategies for planning our time, and also some ways to deal with unexpected interruptions, obstacles, and counterproductive personal habits, especially procrastination. We conclude by turning from relatively short-term considerations to a view of the big picture—the long-term use of time, extending even as far as the entire life span.

Prepare: Knowing Where Time is Going

Before you get somewhere, you need to know where you're starting and where you want to go. So the first step in improving your time management skills is figuring out how you're managing your time now. Complete the *In My Own Words* on the following page to answer the question "Where does my time go?"

Becoming aware of time. Here are some further ways to figure out how you are now spending your time.

- **Create a time log**. "Where did the day go?" If you've ever said this to yourself, you know the feeling of having spent significant blocks of time on…what? Time has passed, but you have no idea of how you spent it.

  One way of figuring out where you've spent your time is to create a **time log**. In fact, a time log is the most basic and essential tool for improving your time management skills.

  A time log is simply a record of how you spend your time. It doesn't have to be a second-by-second record of every waking moment. But it should account for blocks of time in increments as short as 15 minutes.

In My Own Words
Where Does My Time Go?

On the typical weekday, what time do you wake up?

On average, about how much time each day do you spend on the following activities?

    performing your morning routine (i.e., washing up, dressing, grooming, etc.):

    preparing food and eating (including snacks):

    traveling (e.g., between classes):

    hanging out (e.g., chatting informally, except over food):

    exercising:

    in class:

    performing sports, extracurricular, and recreational activities:

    on a job:

    doing school-related work:

    taking care of family members (e.g., children, parents, siblings):

    writing letters or entries in a journal:

    shopping:

    on the telephone:

    on the computer (except for school-related work):

    watching television:

    reading (except for school-related work):

    preparing for bed:

    sleeping:

On the typical weekday, what time do you go to sleep?

Do the above activities add up to a 24-hour day? How do you account for any difference you found?

How hard was it to answer these questions and account for your typical day?

Look at the blank time log in *Try It!* # 1. As you fill out the log, be specific, indicating not only what you were doing at a given time (for example, "reading psychology assignment") but also the interruptions that occurred (such as "answered phone twice" or "switched to Internet for 10 minutes").

Try It! #1
Create a Time Log

Keep track of your days on a log like this one. Be sure to make plenty of copies before you fill it in.

	hygiene	food	classes	studies	work	recreation	personal	sleep	other
A.M. 12:00 15 30 45									
1:00 15 30 45									
2:00 15 30 45									
3:00 15 30 45									
4:00 15 30 45									
5:00 15 30 45									
6:00 15 30 45									
7:00 15 30 45									

	hygiene	food	classes	studies	work	recrea-tion	person-al	sleep	other
8:00 15 30 45									
9:00 15 30 45									
10:00 15 30 45									
11:00 15 30 45									
P.M. 12:00 15 30 45									
1:00 15 30 45									
2:00 15 30 45									
3:00 15 30 45									
4:00 15 30 45									
5:00 15 30 45									
6:00 15 30 45									

	hygiene	food	classes	studies	work	recrea-tion	person-al	sleep	other
7:00 15 30 45									
8:00 15 30 45									
9:00 15 30 45									
10:00 15 30 45									
11:00 15 30 45									

Keep your time log for at least seven days, using a "typical" week. Obviously, no week will be completely typical, but if it's near normal, it will provide you with enough information to give you a good sense of where your time goes.

After your log is complete, analyze how you spend your time according to the major categories on the log. As the example shows, note how much time you spend on (1) hygiene (showering, brushing teeth, eating, etc.), (2) food (cooking, eating, shopping), (3) taking classes, (4) studying, (5) work, (6) recreation and leisure (sports, TV, concerts, exercise), (7) personal (writing, church, family activities), (8) sleep, and (9) anything else that comes up. You can also create other broad categories that eat up significant amounts of time.

Now you know where your time goes. How does it match with your perceptions of how you spend your time? Be prepared to be surprised, because most people find that they're spending time on a lot of activities that just don't matter very much. Many of us, in fact, are hostage to activities and circumstances—we can call them "time terrorists"—that prevent us from doing what we'd rather be doing.

- **Identify the time terrorists in your life**. We're all held hostage by time terrorists, activities that keep us from doing the things that we should be doing and really want to do.

Some time terrorists are beyond our control. For instance, if the bus we take to campus breaks down, and we're forced to wait 40 minutes for another one to come along, there's not much we could have done to prevent it. That's an uncontrollable situation.

But other things are considerably more controllable. For example, suppose when you're studying you get a phone call from a friend, and you end up speaking with her for an hour. This is a case in which you had control over the situation. You could have (a) let the phone ring and not answered it; (b) answered, but told your friend you were studying and promised to call her back; or (c) spoken to her, but only for a short while. If you had done any of these things, you would have taken control of the interruption, and held the time terrorist at bay.

59

- **Set your priorities.** By this point you should have a good idea of what's taking up your time. But you may not know what you should be doing instead.

   To figure out the best use of your time, you need to determine your priorities. **Priorities** are the tasks and activities you need and want to do, rank-ordered from most important to least important. There are no right or wrong priorities; you have to decide for yourself what you wish to accomplish. Maybe spending time on your studies is most important to you, or maybe your top priority is spending time with your family. Only you can decide. Furthermore, what's important to you at this moment may be less of a priority to you next month, next year, or five years from now.

   For the purpose of effective time management in college, the best procedure is to start off by identifying priorities for an entire term. What do you need to accomplish? Don't just choose obvious, general goals, such as "passing all my classes." Instead, think about your priorities in terms of specific, measurable activities, such as "studying ten hours before each psychology exam."

   Write your priorities on a chart. After you've filled out the chart, organize it by giving each priority a "priority index" number from 1 to 3. A "1" represents a priority that absolutely must be done; without it you'll suffer a major setback. For instance, a paper with a fixed due date is a number 1 priority; carving out time to take those guitar lessons you always wanted to take might be a number 3 priority. The important point is to rank order your priorities to reveal what is and is not important to accomplish during the term.

   Setting priorities will help you to determine how to make best use of your time. No one has enough time to complete everything; prioritizing will help you make informed decisions about what you can do to maximize your success.

- **Know when you're in prime time.** Each of us has our own style based on some innate internal clock. Some of us are at our best in the morning, while others do considerably better at night. Being aware of your optimal period of functioning will help you plan and schedule your time most effectively. If you're at your worst in the morning, try to schedule easier, less involving activities. On the other hand, if morning is the best time for you, schedule activities that require the greatest concentration.

   But don't be a slave to your internal time clock. Even night people can function effectively in the morning, just as morning people can accomplish quite a bit in the evening. Don't let your concerns become a self-fulfilling prophecy.

Organize: Mastering the Moment

   Your time management preparation has brought you to a point where you now know where you've lost time in the past. Furthermore, your priority list is telling you where you need to be headed in the future.

   Now for the present. You've reached the point where you can organize yourself to take control of your time. Here's what you'll need:

- A **master calendar** that shows all the weeks of the term on one page. You don't need to buy one; you can make it easily enough yourself using a piece of posterboard. It need not be Great Art; a rough version will do. The important point is that it must include every week of the term and seven days per week.
- A **weekly timetable**. The weekly timetable is a master grid with the days of the week across the top and the hours, from 6:00 a.m. to 12:00 midnight, along the side. This will permit you to write in all your regularly scheduled activities, as well as one-time appointments as they arise.
- A **daily to-do list**. Finally, you'll need a daily to-do list. The to-do list can be written on a small, portable calendar that includes a separate page for each day of the week. Or it can simply be a small notebook, with a separate sheet of paper for every day of the week. Whatever form your

daily to-do list takes, you'll need to keep it with you all the time, so make sure it's not too cumbersome.

The basic organizational task you face is filling in these three schedules. You'll need at least an hour to do this, so set the time aside. There will be some repetition across the three schedules, and the task may seem a bit tedious. But keep this in mind: Without a doubt, every minute you invest now in organizing your time will pay off in hours that you will save in the future. Time management is an investment with a better (and safer!) rate of return than anything you'll find in the stock market.

Follow these steps in completing your schedule:

- Start with the **master calendar** that shows all the weeks of the term on one page. In most classes, you'll receive a syllabus, a course outline that explains what the course is all about. Traditionally, a syllabus includes course assignments and their due dates, and the schedule for tests that will be given during the term. Write on the master calendar *every* assignment you have, noting it on the date that it is due. If the instructor hasn't included due dates, ask; he or she probably already knows, or at least has a general idea, of the week that various assignments will be due. Pencil in tentative assignments on the appropriate date.

   Don't put only assignments on the master calendar. Also include important activities from your personal life, drawn from your list of priorities. For instance, if you're involved in a club that is bringing a guest speaker to campus, mark down the date of the event. Finally, schedule some free days—days when you promise yourself you will do something that is just plain fun. Consider these days inviolate—promise yourself that you'll permit no sudden event to snatch them away.

   You now have a good idea of what the term has in store for you. In most cases, the first few weeks have few assignments or tests. But as the term rolls on—particularly around the middle and end of the term—things will get more demanding. The message you should take from this: Use the off-peak periods to get a head start on assignments that are due in the future.

- Now move to the **weekly timetable**. Start by filling in the times of all your fixed, prescheduled activities—the times that your classes meet, when you have to be at work, the times you have to pick up your daughter at day care, and any other recurring appointments.

   Once you've filled in your weekly timetable, you can get a sense of what your "average" week will be like. But this is just a bare bones picture of the average week, because you will also need to take into account the specific activities that are required to complete the assignments on the master calendar.

   To move from your "average" week to specific weeks, make photocopies of the weekly timetable that now contains your fixed appointments. Make enough copies for every week of the term. On each copy write the week number of the term and the specific dates it covers.

   Using your master calendar, add assignment due dates, tests, and any other activities on the appropriate days of the week. Then pencil in blocks of time necessary to prepare for those events.

   How much time should you allocate for school work? One rule of thumb is that every one hour that you spend in class requires, on average, another two hours of study outside of class. Do the arithmetic: If you're taking 15 credits (with each credit equivalent to an hour of class), you'll need to plan for 30 hours of studying each week—a daunting amount of time. Of course, the amount of time you must allocate to a specific class will vary from week to week, depending on what is happening in the class.

   If you estimate that you'll need five hours of study for a midterm exam in a certain class, pencil in those hours. Don't set up a single block of five hours, though. As we discussed in the previous chapter on memory, people remember best when their studying is spread out over shorter periods rather than attempted in one long block of time.

   Similarly, if you need to write a paper that's due on a certain date, you can block out the different stages of the writing process (described in Chapter 3). You'll need to estimate how much time each stage will take, but you probably have a pretty good idea from previous papers you've written.

Keep in mind that estimates are just that: estimates. Don't think of them as set in stone. Mark them on your weekly calendar in pencil, not pen, so you can adjust them if necessary.

But remember: it's also crucial not to overschedule yourself. You'll still need time to eat, to talk with your friends, to spend time with your family, and in general to enjoy yourself. If you find that your life is completely filled with things that you feel you must do in order to survive, and there is no room for fun, then take a step back. Extract some time for yourself from your daily schedule. Finding time for yourself is as important as carving out time for what others want you to do.

- If you've taken each of the previous steps, you're now in a position to work on the final bit of preparation for successful time management: completing your **daily to-do list**.

Unlike the master calendar and weekly timetable—both of which you develop at the beginning of the term—you shouldn't work on your daily to-do list far in advance. In fact, the best approach is to complete it just one day ahead of time, preferably at the end of the day.

List all the things that you intend to do during the next day. Start with the things you know you must do that have fixed times, such as classes, work schedules, and appointments. Then add in the other things that you need to accomplish, such as an hour of study for an upcoming test; working on research for an upcoming paper; or finishing up a lab report. Finally, list things that are enjoyable—a time-out for a run or a walk.

The idea is not to schedule every single minute of the day. That would be counterproductive, and you'd end up feeling like you'd failed if you deviated from your schedule. Instead, think of your daily to-do list as a path through a forest that you are following on a hike. As on a hike, you should allow yourself to deviate from the path, taking occasional forays onto side tracks when they look interesting.

Like the daily to-do list illustrated on the following page, include a column to check off after you've completed an activity. There's nothing so satisfying as a completed to-do list bedecked with check marks.

To-Do List

- ✓ Methods class
- ✓ meet Lisa for lunch
- ✓ work from 3-6
- ✓ study for Physio quiz—1hr
  read Developmental Chapter 4
- ✓ start writing intro for 1ˢᵗ methods project
- ✓ get home for Melrose at 9pm

Work: Controlling Time

There is no work to time management.

Well, not exactly. But time management is largely about preparation and organization; the work itself involves completing the activities that you need and wish to complete. If you've prepared and organized carefully, you'll be ready to complete your work.

In short, the work of time management is to follow the schedules that you've put together. But that doesn't mean it will be easy. Our lives are filled with surprises. Things take longer than we'd planned. A friend we haven't spoken to in a while calls to chat, and it seems rude to say that we don't have time to talk. A crisis occurs: Buses are late, computers break down, kids get sick.

The difference between effective time management and time management that doesn't work lies in dealing with the surprises. There are several ways to take control of your days and permit yourself to follow your intended schedule:

- **Just say no.** You don't have to agree to every request and every favor that others ask of you. You're not a bad person if you refuse to do something that will eat up your time and prevent you from accomplishing your goals.

- **Get away from it all.** Go to the library. Lock yourself into your bedroom. Find an out-of-the-way unused classroom.

  Any of these places can serve to isolate you from everyday distractions, and thereby permit you to work on the tasks that you wish to complete. Try to adopt a particular spot as your own, such as a corner desk in a secluded nook in the library. If you use it enough, your body and mind will automatically get into "study" mode as soon as you seat yourself at it.

- **Enjoy the sounds of silence.** Although many students insist they accomplish most while a television, radio, or CD is playing, scientific studies suggest otherwise: We are able to concentrate most when our environment is silent. So even if you're sure you work best with a sound track playing, try an experiment and work in silence for several days. You may find that you're more efficient and accomplish more in a shorter time than in a noisy environment.

- **Take control of your communications.** The telephone. E-mail. Regular mail. Who doesn't love to receive messages from others?

  The problem is that we don't control when those communications arrive—they are in the hands of others. And despite the fact that they may come at inconvenient times, they have power that says, "Answer me! This might be interesting! This may be the message you've been waiting for."

  The reality is this: Every message you receive, no matter what the form, can wait until you're ready to receive it. Telephone calls can be stored on answering machines or voice-mail systems; e-mail can be saved on a computer; and regular mail can sit in a mailbox. If you wait until *you* have the time to take a message, you'll be able to follow your time management plans far better.

- **Let your fingers do the walking.** As an old telephone company advertisement for the yellow pages says, "Let your fingers do the walking." Many things can be done over the phone—or via e-mail or voice mail—rather than in person. It is much faster to call the bank to check on your bank balance than it is to walk over, stand in line, and finally get waited on.

- **Expect the unexpected.** Interruptions and crises, minor and major, can't be eliminated. However, they can be prepared for. By making sure your schedule has some slack in it, you'll have the opportunity to regain time lost to unexpected events.

  Even more important, try to anticipate the unanticipated. How is it possible to plan for surprises? Take a look at the time log you created earlier in the chapter, and think about what you've already encountered in your courses during the current term. What sorts of unexpected occurrences suddenly require your attention? Do they tend to involve a particular kind of event or a particular person?

  You'll never be able to escape from unexpected interruptions and surprises that require your attention. But by trying to anticipate them in advance, and thinking about how you'll react to them, you'll be positioning yourself to react more effectively when they do occur.

- **Don't procrastinate.** You can't control interruptions and crises that are foisted upon you by others. But even when no one else is throwing interruptions at us, some of us make up our own. **Procrastination**, the habit of putting off and delaying tasks that are to be accomplished, is a problem that many of us face. (To identify whether you are a procrastinator, find your "Procrastination Quotient" in the accompanying *Try It!* exercise.)

Try It! #2
Are You a Procrastinator?

Do you procrastinate?[1] Check off which of the following apply to you:

	Strongly agree	Mildly agree	Mildly disagree	Strongly disagree
1. I invent reasons and look for excuses for not acting on a problem				
2. It takes pressure to get me to work on difficult assignments.				
3. I take half measures that will avoid or delay unpleasant or difficult tasks.				
4. I face too many interruptions and crises that interfere with my accomplishing my major goals.				
5. I sometimes neglect to carry out important tasks.				
6. I schedule big assignments too late to get them done as well as I know I could.				
7. I'm sometimes too tired to do the work I need to do.				
8. I start new tasks before I finish old ones.				
9. When I work in groups, I try to get other people to finish what I don't.				
10. I put off tasks that I really don't want to do but know that I must do.				
Scoring: Total up responses in each column:				
Multiply them by this number:	x 4	x 3	x 2	X 1
Put the multiplied score here:				

Add up your scores. If the score is below 20, you're not a chronic procrastinator and you probably have only an occasional problem. If your score is 21–30, you have a minor problem with procrastination. If your score is above 30, you should work on procrastination, because it is a style that you use relatively often.

If you are diligent in applying the time management techniques that we've been discussing, procrastination should be minimized. But what if you find yourself procrastinating? Several steps can help you:

- ❑ **Break large tasks into small ones.** People often procrastinate because a task they're seeking to accomplish appears overwhelming. If writing a 15-page paper seems nearly impossible, think about writing a series of five 3-page papers. If reading a 750-page book seems impossible, think of it as reading several 250-page books.

- **Start with the easiest and simplest part of a task, and then do the harder parts.** Succeeding initially on the easy parts can make the harder parts of a task less daunting—and make you less apt to procrastinate in completing the task.
- **Work with others.** Working with others who must accomplish the same task as you can help prevent procrastination. Just being in the same physical location with others can motivate you sufficiently to accomplish tasks that you consider unpleasant and on which you might be tempted to procrastinate. Beware, though: If you spend too much time socializing, you lower the likelihood of success.
- **Keep the costs of procrastination in mind.** Procrastination doesn't just result in delay. It may also make the task harder than it would have been if you hadn't procrastinated. Not only will you ultimately have less time to complete the task, but you may have to do it so quickly that its quality may be diminished. In the worst scenario, you won't even be able to finish it at all.

Evaluate: Time Checks

Evaluation of time management is considerably more straightforward than in most other domains: You either accomplished what you intended to do in a given period, or you didn't. The way to determine how well you succeeded is to check off each item that you have accomplished on your daily to-do list. Try to do this at the end of every day. If you do it then, not only will you know how successful your management efforts have been, but you will be able to incorporate any activities you missed into the next day's to-do list.

Of course, you won't always accomplish every item on your to-do list. That's not surprising, nor even particularly bad, especially if you've included some second- and third-level priorities that you don't absolutely have to accomplish, and which you may not really have expected you'd have time for anyway.

As you evaluate your success at time management, it's important to focus on more than your daily priorities. You should take a longer view. Even if you are regularly completing everything you intended to accomplish on a given day—and that's no small achievement—you need to consider the big picture of your life.

Some of the most important things in life have no urgent deadlines. We need to take time out to enjoy our friends, admire the flowers in the park, spend some "nonsense time" with our children, exercise, consider the spiritual side of our lives. None of these activities present themselves as having an immediate deadline. Yet they are vital to our well-being. In fact, in the long run, our success as human beings may be more dependent on these less time-bound goals than on goals with imminent deadlines.

Finally, it's important to remember the inexorable nature of time: It never stops. Regardless of how well—or how poorly—we've done in time management for one day, tomorrow is another day. That realization may be either a challenge or a relief. Whatever we did today, tomorrow we can wipe the slate clean, develop another to-do list, and start afresh. The time will always be there: We just have to make sure we're using it correctly.

Rethink: Having the Time of Your Life

At the end of the day, after you've evaluated how well you've followed your time management plan and how much you've accomplished, it's time to rethink where you are. Maybe you've accomplished everything you set out to do, and every task for the day is completed, and every item on your to-do list has a checkmark next to it.

Or maybe you have the opposite result. Your day has been a shambles, and you feel as if nothing has been accomplished. Because of a constant series of interruptions and chance events, you've been unable to make headway on your list.

Or—most likely—you find yourself somewhere in between these two extremes. Some tasks got done, while others are still hanging over you.

No matter what the outcome, it's time neither to panic nor to sit back and applaud yourself (yet). Instead, spend some time rethinking your priorities and your time management strategies by doing the following:

- **Consider your personal style of time management.** We've outlined one method of time management. Although it works well for most people, it isn't for everyone. Some people just can't bring themselves to be so structured and scheduled, feeling hemmed in by to-do lists.

  If you're one of the those people, fine. You don't need to follow the suggestions presented in this chapter. But you do need to follow *some* time management strategy. Perhaps it might consist of jotting down due dates, and then each day looking at them and figuring out what to do that day. Perhaps it might consist of visualizing your completion of tasks, and using that visualization to guide your behavior each day. Or perhaps it might mean working on assignments as soon as you get them. Rather than waiting until the last minute, you try to accomplish them as soon as you know they need to be done.

  Whatever approach to time management you choose, make sure you have one. And be certain that it is compatible with your own personal values and strengths. Keep experimenting until you find an approach that works for you.

- **Do less.** If you consistently fall behind in your work, it may be that you are just doing too much. Reassess your goals and your priorities, and make choices. Determine what is most important to you. It's better to accomplish less, if it is accomplished well, than to accomplish more, but poorly.

- **Do more.** If you consistently accomplish everything you want to do and still have time on your hands, do more. Although it is a problem that many of us would envy, some people have too much time on their hands. Their classes may not be too demanding, or work demands may suddenly slacken off. Or perhaps a child for whom they are caring begins to attend public school full time. In such situations, they may suddenly feel like their life is proceeding at a more leisurely pace than before.

  If this happens to you, there are several responses you might consider. One is to simply relax. If it's only a temporary respite, take it easy for a term and enjoy a more unhurried existence.

  On the other hand, if you consistently have more time than you know what to do with, rethink how to make use of your time. Reflect on what you want to accomplish with your life, and add some activities that help you reach your goals. For example, consider becoming involved in an extracurricular activity. Think about volunteering your time to needy individuals and organizations. Consider taking an extra course during the next term.

  But whatever you decide to do, make it a decision. Don't let the time slip away.

- **Take a long view of time.** One danger of time management is that it may lead you to focus on the short term. If you only think in terms of minutes and hours—or even days, you risk forgetting about your really long-term goals and values.

  Time management is not about schedules and clocks and to-do lists. Instead, it's about permitting you to take control of your life. It's about choices that you make, rather than choices that others make for you. It's about taking charge.

  Consequently, it is essential to know what's important to you and what you wish to accomplish in the time that you'll have over your lifetime. One way is to make a timeline of your life, as in the *Try It!* exercise on the following page.

Try It! #3
Create a Life Timeline

To create a life timeline, think about what you'd like to accomplish over the course of your life. Consider accomplishments in many realms, including career, family, social, service, spiritual, financial, and leisure. Below is a sample timeline. Feel free to copy it and complete it. You may want to return to it every few years and see how you're doing.

Life Timeline

Date:

Realm	Age											
	25	30	35	40	45	50	55	60	65	70	75	80
Career												
Family												
Social												
Service												
Spiritual												
Financial												
Leisure												

67

WEB P.O.W.E.R.

Study Time
1) http://www.coun.uvic.ca/learn/program/hndouts/plan_html
This site provides effective hints on how to plan study time, ideas about when to study, as well as tips on how to study.

Self-Management Checklist
2) http://www.coun.uvic.ca/learn/program/hndouts/slfman.html
This site provides a handy self-management checklist that allows visitors to better achieve their goals with the time that they have. It also provides effective techniques for avoiding procrastination and digression, two major obstacles to effective time management.

Planning for Goals
3) http://www.mindtools.com/page5.html
The focus of this site is how to get the most out of one's time. Topics covered include analyzing what time is really worth, prioritizing goals, and planning effective use of the time that one actually has.

---

[1] Adapted from Ferner, J.D. 1980. *Successful Time Management.* New York, NY: Wiley, 33.

Chapter 6

Information Management

Melissa Fisher had become a psychology major because of a condition she'd developed when she was 13. At that time Melissa had experienced her first seizure—hearing voices and seeing colors that weren't there and losing physical control over her body. Her doctors identified her condition as temporal lobe epilepsy and prescribed medication, and her seizures became less frequent.

Even though she hadn't had a seizure in six years, Melissa felt somewhat isolated and different from other students. She had a few close friends, but she lived in fear that she would have a seizure at school. She'd really wanted to join the university choir, but she ended up not even trying out because she worried that if she had a seizure during a rehearsal, no one there would be able to help her.

But when Melissa began researching the topic of epilepsy for her Neuropsych class, her world opened up. On the World Wide Web, Melissa discovered chat rooms and listservs devoted to people with the same type of epilepsy she had. These people mentioned having many of the fears that she did, but they also had a lot more information about how to deal with those fears. Having others to talk to helped Melissa gain the confidence to make new friends on campus and she eventually joined the choir. Suddenly she didn't feel quite so different and alone.

Looking Ahead

The world of information is growing at breakneck speed. Each day, tens of thousands of books and scientific articles are published. We're exposed to more information in a year than our grandparents were exposed to in their entire lifetimes. Scientific knowledge doubles every seven years.

But such statistics pale in light of the power that information has to change our lives. Although the result isn't always as dramatic as the knowledge found by Melissa Fisher, the increased availability of information does provide an opportunity to grow and expand our understanding of ourselves and others.

In this chapter we discuss **information management**—the ability to find, harness, and use knowledge. We'll consider information found in traditional libraries and in the virtual world of cyberspace. We'll examine how to find what we need in books and magazines and through the World Wide Web.

As we begin our journey down what has been called the information superhighway, fasten your seatbelt and get ready for the ride of your life. It's a wild ride, one with frequent twists and turns, dark alleyways, false trails, and an ever-changing terrain. But it will take you places you've never been before, exposing you to information that will open your eyes to ideas, sights, and sounds that you never dreamed existed. We'll begin the journey by taking stock of our possessions and packing the gear that will be essential.

Prepare: Honing Your Information Survival Skills

Before you set out into the world of information, you need to do a few things to ready yourself— consider them survival skills for the trip ahead. As with an ascent of Mount Everest, the better prepared you are, the more likely you are to succeed. The most important skills you'll need are the following:

- **Learn basic computer skills.** You weren't born knowing how to use a pencil. When you were in elementary school, your teachers had to teach you how to do it. You had to learn the right way to hold the pencil, how to position it so it would work most effectively, and how to produce the letters that make up writing. You learned to do it, of course, and now it hardly seems worth thinking about.

In My Own Words
How Do I Feel About Computers?

In general, what are your feelings about computers? Are they closer to fear or love?

Which of the Seven Deadly Sins apply to your feelings about computers (circle all that apply): pride, anger, envy, lust, gluttony, greed, or sloth?

When confronted with a computer, which of Snow White's companions do you most resemble: Sleepy, Sneezy, Doc, Dopey, Happy, Grumpy, or Bashful?

In your view, how likely are computers to be helpful in completing routine tasks associated with college work?

How likely are computers to fail and in some way mess up or complicate routine tasks?

How would you characterize your level of computer expertise: very low, low, moderate, high, very high?

How would you characterize your level of computer use: very low, low, moderate, high, very high?

Would you like to know more about computers? Would you like to use them more often?

For what sorts of tasks do you find computers indispensable?

For what sorts of tasks do you consider computers useless?

What was your worst experience with a computer?

Although it's impossible to learn basic computer skills without access to a computer—just as it would be hard to learn how to use a pencil without having one available—there are certain things you should know before you seat yourself in front of a computer:

- **Computer hardware.** The **hardware** of a computer consists of the parts that you see: the monitor (or screen), keyboard, mouse, and "system unit," the box-like object that includes the computer's memory, disk drives, and other components (sometimes also referred to as the CPU—central processing unit). The hardware sits in a state of readiness, waiting to carry out instructions. It is similar to a brainless human body—ready to function, but immobile without the brain's orders.

- **Computer software.** The **software** of a computer, which comes in the form of different kinds of *programs*, tells the computer what to do by providing a sequence of instructions. Or, rather, it allows *you* to tell the computer what to do. Computer hardware can't do anything without software telling it what it should be doing.

- **Learn to use the Internet.** Be prepared: If you haven't already become acquainted with the Internet, your first encounter with it may change your life.

  The **Internet** is a network connecting millions of computers together. Its immense "interconnectedness" permits a user to share information with virtually anyone else who has a computer. The resources available to users are vast; from your home desktop you can have access to information stored nearly anywhere around the globe. In fact, that's an understatement: Live images from as far away as the planet Mars have been transmitted to users via the Internet.

  Because the Internet is constantly evolving, the best place to learn about it is on the Internet itself. Here are a few of the features that you are most likely to find useful:

  - **E-mail.** The most widely used feature of the Internet is **e-mail**, short for "electronic mail." E-mail offers a way for people to send messages to one another instantly, and to receive replies rapidly. On some college campuses, almost all faculty use e-mail. For students, e-mail is an increasingly convenient way to contact instructors.

  - **Telnet.** Using **telnet,** a dial-up communication system that permits users at remote locations to use computer databases and other resources housed on distant computers, a computer in one location can act as if it were present in another. For example, you may be able to access the card catalog of a university library across the country just as if you were sitting at a terminal in the library itself.

  - **Bulletin boards and newsgroups.** The Internet contains thousands of electronic "areas" where people can read and post messages and news relevant to a particular topic. For example, there are bulletin boards and **newsgroups** devoted to the stock market, snowmobiles, *Party of Five*, the Boston Celtics, the Spice Girls, and Shakespeare's sonnets.

  - **Listserv Groups.** A **listserv** is a subscription service through which members can post and receive messages via e-mail on general topics of shared interest. A listserv automatically distributes messages via e-mail to people who have added their names to the listserv's mailing list. Individuals can respond to messages by replying to the listserv, and their responses will be distributed automatically to everyone on the mailing list.

  - **World Wide Web.** The **World Wide Web** is a highly graphical—even multimedia—means of accessing information on the Internet. The Web is rapidly becoming the standard interface between the Internet and those who wish to use its resources. As we'll consider later, the Web provides a way to transmit not just typewritten text but pictorial information—such as graphs, photos, and video clips—and even audio information as well.

- **Acquaint yourself with information storehouses.** The world contains a tremendous amount of information. To use it, you've got to know where it's kept. In general, you'll find information stored in two distinct kinds of places, and you need to familiarize yourself with both of them. One you can walk or drive to—the traditional library—while the other doesn't even have a physical location—computer information networks. Both are indispensable in guiding you in your quest for information.

  - ❑ **Libraries.** Libraries are meant to provide us with a way to find answers to our questions, to learn new ways of looking at the world, to identify what others before us have thought, and to obtain the keys that will permit us to enter the minds of others.

    Although every library is different, all share some basic characteristics. Specifically, libraries all contain the following key components:

    - ❖ **Basic collections.** It's surely not surprising that a library would contain books. But they typically contain a lot more than that. They have periodicals—magazines, journals, and newspapers that are published on a recurring basis. Some libraries also store government documents, CDs and records, and musical scores. Some have **microform** collections in which documents (such as old issues of newspapers or magazines) that have been photographed and greatly reduced in size are stored on either microfilm (reels of film) or microfiche (plastic sheets) that can be read with special microform readers. Larger libraries also may contain rare books which are stored in separate rooms, that require special permission to use.

      Many college libraries contain reserve collections. Reserve collections hold heavily used items that instructors assign for a class. Sometimes reserve material can be checked out for only an hour or two and used in the same room; in other cases the material can be used overnight or for a few days.

    - ❖ **Catalogs.** A catalog is a listing of all materials that are held in the library. Traditionally, catalogs consisted of paper cards that were filed in trays. In large libraries, the card catalog sometimes extended across several huge rooms. Today, however, the catalogs of an increasing number of libraries are computerized. Rather than physically sorting through cards, users conduct a catalog search on a computer. Computerized catalogs may be accessible from home computers as well as from computers housed in the library itself.

      Other libraries use microform media, either microfiche or microfilm, for their catalogs. And many libraries are in transition, using a combination of forms. Whatever way the information is physically stored, it usually has the same characteristics. Specifically, the information is sorted by title, author name, and subject. Individual entries generally include additional information, such as the publisher, date of publication, and similar information pertaining to the item.

    - ❖ **Indexes.** How can you find articles published in magazines, newspapers, and journals? Indexes are the answer. An index provides a listing of journal articles by subject area and author. Some indexes also provide a short summary, or **abstract,** of the contents of each article.

      Indexes come in both book and computerized form. Although some people prefer to use indexes in book form, computerized indexes are considerably easier and quicker to use.

    - ❖ **Encyclopedias.** Encyclopedias provide a broad overview of knowledge. Some, such as the *Encyclopaedia Britannica* or *World Book Encyclopedia* attempt to cover the entire range of knowledge, and they may take up several volumes. Others are more specialized, covering only a particular field, such as the *Encyclopedia of Human Behavior* or the *Encyclopedia of Religion*. Most are printed as multivolume sets of books, although an increasing number come in computerized versions.

Although encyclopedias can provide a good overview of a topic, they lack depth. Furthermore, because they are not revised frequently (at least in printed form), they may be out of date by the time you use them. Still, their breadth offers an important advantage: they provide a general, overall view of a topic, raising key issues that can lead the user to more specific and current sources.

❑ **The World Wide Web.** Want to know where to get a haircut in Dubuque, Iowa? The telephone number of your favorite author? The opening theme of Schubert's Unfinished Symphony? The date on which the space shuttle *Challenger* exploded?

The place to look for all this information is the same: the World Wide Web, or—for short—the Web. As we noted earlier, the Web is a computer resource that links a vast array of information to the user's computer terminal. The information may be text, photos, graphs, video clips, or musical selections.

Like a library, the Web involves several essential components. They are:

❖ **Browser.** In order to use the World Wide Web, you need a computer that contains a browser. A **browser** is a program that provides a way of navigating around the information on the Web. Among the major browsers are Netscape Navigator and Microsoft Internet Explorer.

To use a browser, you indicate the location of the information that you're seeking by typing in an address. Web addresses are odd combinations of letters and symbols. They typically start off with "http://www" and then go on from there. In and of themselves the letters and symbols have relatively little meaning, in the same way that knowing that people live at 348 Elm Street doesn't inform you if they have an elm tree in front of their house. What the address does is simply identify a unique location on the Web, known as a *Web page* (or sometimes *Web site*), that you are directing your browser to find.

❖ **Web pages.** Also known as Web sites, Web pages are the heart of the World Wide Web. A **Web page** is a location on the World Wide Web that presents you with information. The information may appear as text on the screen, to be read like a book (or more accurately, like an ancient scroll). Or it might be a video clip, an audio clip, a photo, a portrait, a graph, or a figure. It may be a news service photo of the president of the United States or a backyard snapshot of someone's family reunion. There is as much variety in the kinds of information available to you on the Web as there is variety in people.

❖ **Links.** Information at a particular site typically provides you with **links**—a means of automatically "jumping"—to other Web pages. Just as an encyclopedia article on forests might say at the end, "See also "Trees," Web pages often provide a means of reaching other sites on the Web—only it's easier than with a book.

Web pages highlight links to other pages, usually by presenting them as underlined text in a different color. To reach the link, the user clicks on the link with the computer mouse, and the browser automatically moves to the Web page of the link.

❖ **Search engine. Search engine** is simply another name for a computerized index to information on the Web. Among the most popular are Yahoo!, Alta Vista, and Excite!

Search engines themselves are located on the Web, so you have to know their addresses to make them work for you. After you reach the specific Web address of a search engine, you will be prompted to enter the topic of the search. The search engine then provides a list of possible Web sites that contain the relevant information. You can then scan the list and check out the most relevant sites.

Like library catalogs, search engines can locate specific information for you. Unlike library catalogs, search engines do not provide a complete record of everything that it is housed on the Web. In fact, no one knows how much material exists and where every bit of it is located. Not only is more information added to the Internet every day, but the information resides on thousands of individual computers. Virtually anyone with a computer can set up an individual, personal Web site.

Having introduced the major sources of information that permit us to prepare for the process of obtaining information, it's time to move forward. We turn, then, to the next stage of information management: organizing.

Try It! #1
Information, Please!

To find information efficiently, you have to have a pretty good idea where to turn first. See if you can match the following questions with the information source that would most likely provide the answer.

Question	Information Source
1. What is the Structuralist Approach to psychology and when was it introduced?	A. Almanac
2. What are the titles of some recent books by E. O. Wilson?	B. World Wide Web
3. What review did Philip Lieberman's latest book receive from the New York Times?	C. Dictionary
4. What are the words of Dr. Martin Luther King, Jr.'s "I Have a Dream" speech?	D. Encyclopedia
5. Who won the 1979 Pulitzer Prize for general nonfiction writing?	E. Library Catalog
6. Where can I find some recent magazine articles on circadian rhythms?	F. Library Microform Collection
7. What is a synapse?	G. Reader's Guide to Periodic Literature

Answers: 1D; 2E; 3F; 4B; 5A; 6G; 7C.

Organize: Narrowing Your Search

The biggest information management task most people face is not the task of finding information. Instead, after taking advantage of the library and Web, many people have just the opposite problem: They end up with *too much* information.

How people organize what they've found often marks the difference between success and failure. Keep in mind these tips for organizing information effectively:

- **Determine what you're looking for.** Suppose you have to write a paper for your developmental psychology class, and because you've always been interested in language development, you decide to write about it. You go to the library card catalog and find that your college has many dozens of books about language development. You take a look at the

World Wide Web and the situation is even worse, with literally thousands of references to language development. What do you do next?

You need to refine your topic, transforming it from a broad, open-ended universe of content to a more restricted, manageable domain of ideas and information. Look at a few of the sources you've found and consider the major issues surrounding language development. Perhaps some of the books have chapters on particular subtopics, such as the development of first words or how children learn the rules of conversation. Because these questions are more restricted and targeted, they make a more manageable topic for a paper.

- **Identify the key sources of information.** Every field has experts, and you need to make sure that you consider what they have said about your topic. How do you identify the experts? One way is to read through several books and see whose names keep popping up. Another way is to use an encyclopedia to get an overview of your topic. Encyclopedia articles often end with suggested readings; these can guide you to the appropriate sources of information.

- **Keep in mind what you're going to do with the information.** As you begin to do your research, keep your goal in mind. Are you writing a short, 2-page position paper? A longer term paper? A speech? A worksheet? Knowing what you need to do with the information will help you to organize your information search.

- **Learn the key issues and controversies involving your topic.** Every field has key issues and certain controversies that remain unresolved. Identifying what these issues and controversies are from the earliest stages of your research will ensure that you cover what is important. They can also make the assignment you're seeking to complete—whether it's a paper, a speech, or a report—far more interesting than a mere recitation of facts.

- **Use librarians effectively.** Make use of librarians—but do it properly. Don't ask vague, unfocused questions (e.g., "Where are the books about child development?"). Instead, sharpen your question, being as precise as possible ("I'm writing a paper on the relationship between language and thought in toddlers. What's the best place to look for information?"). But if you really are unsure of how to proceed, don't be bashful. Go ahead and approach a librarian; as information management specialists, they can often offer good suggestions to help you shape your topic and save hours of aimless wandering in an increasingly dense forest of information.

Work: Digging In

Now that you have become acquainted with the basic information management tools, you're in a position to do the actual research. We have already discussed (in Chapter 3) a procedure for recording and organizing information using 3" x 5" note cards, and you might want to review that chapter. Here we'll concentrate on techniques for actually using the tools we've discussed.

- **Using card and computer catalogs.** Catalogs provide a conceptual roadmap to the location of everything in the library. Although it takes some effort to understand how to use a library's catalog—every catalog is slightly different—there are some basic procedures that you can follow:

  - **Searching the catalog.** Although traditional card catalogs (consisting of records of information on actual cards) and computer catalogs (consisting of electronic records) are physically very different, the basic information each contains is the same. Each book (or other library holding) actually can be found in three different ways: by searching by author (*author listing*), by title (*title listing*), and by subject (*subject listing*).

    Each book has a **call number**, a classification unique to a book that tells you where to find it. Most college libraries use the Library of Congress classification system for call numbers, a combination of letters and numbers. The first letter indicates a general topical area, and the numbers provide further classification information. But you don't need to know the system; all that's really important is that it pinpoints the book's location in the library.

❑ **Finding what you need.** Once you've identified a source that looks promising, don't stop there. Keep searching for additional material that may be relevant. You won't know for sure what is and isn't useful until you've actually viewed the material, so don't give up too early.

With your call numbers in hand, it's time to find the actual, physical material that may be helpful. In all but the biggest libraries, you can simply go into the **stacks,** the place containing shelves where the books and other materials are kept, and—using the call number—find what you're looking for. In some cases, however, you won't be permitted to enter the stacks. In libraries with closed stacks, you must fill out a form with the call numbers of the books you want. A library aide will find and deliver the material to a central location.

What if you go to the location in the stacks where the material is supposed to be and you can't find it? The most likely explanation is that the material is checked out by another library patron or in use by someone else at that time. It may also be incorrectly shelved or simply lost. Whatever the reason, don't give up. If the material is checked out to another user, ask the librarian if you can **recall** the material, a process by which the library contacts whoever has the book and asks him or her to return it because someone else needs to use it.

If the librarian informs you that the material is not checked out to someone else, wait a few days and see if it appears on the shelf. Someone may have been using it while you were looking for it, and then left it to be reshelved. If it was misshelved, the librarian may be able to find it. If the material is truly lost, you may be able to get it from another library through **interlibrary loan,** a system by which libraries share resources, making them available to patrons of different libraries. Ask the librarian for help; an interlibrary loan will take some time—between a few days and several weeks—but eventually you'll be able to get the material.

Finally, even if you do find exactly what you were looking for, take a moment to scan the shelves for related material. Because books and other materials are generally grouped by topic on library shelves, you may find something else worth reading. One of the pleasures of libraries is the possibility of finding on the shelves an unexpected treasure—material that your catalog search did not initially identify, but which may provide you with exactly the kind of information you need.

• **Searching the World Wide Web.** Using the World Wide Web to find information couldn't be easier—or more difficult. The ease of navigation around the Web makes finding information quite simple. At the same time, though, the mass of information that is tied into the Web can make finding *appropriate* information harder than locating the proverbial needle in a haystack.

Most of what you will come across may well be of little use. In fact, it's easy to end up in a virtual dead end, in which the information you have found is only minimally related to the topic you're researching. In that case, use the "Back" command on the browser, which will allow you to retrace the route that led to the site in which you currently find yourself.

The other danger with Web searches is that you may come across information that is so fascinating that you stray off-track and lose sight of what you should be doing. It's important, then, keep in mind what you're supposed to be doing and resist the temptations that the Web offers.

x

Try It! #2
Working the Web

Use the World Wide Web to locate information about perception and illusions. If you're doing it right, you should encounter information about depth cues, figure/ground ambiguity, size constancy, the Poggendorf Illusion, Hermann von Helmoltz, the Muller-Lyer Illusion, the Ames Room, and the Ponzo Illusion.

Gather what you found, including source documents, bibliographies, interesting links, and dead ends (you are sure to find some strange things out there!).

Evaluate your overall satisfaction with using the World Wide Web for research on this topic.

- **Avoiding plagiarism.** There's no greater sin in the world of academics than **plagiarism,** taking credit for someone else's words, thoughts, or ideas. In the academic world, plagiarism is about the same as stealing a stranger's car. Even if you just mean to "borrow" a passage, passing another person's work off as your own is totally wrong.

  Furthermore, if you do plagiarize and get caught, the penalty can be severe: In many colleges, plagiarism results in dismissal. You could even face legal charges, because almost all published material is copyrighted, which means that it is someone's "intellectual property." If an author learns that you have used his or her writing as your own, the author has the right to take you to court and sue for damages.

  The best way to deal with the threats that plagiarism raises is to be scrupulous while doing your research. Make sure that everything you write down is put into your own words, except for direct quotes. And when you quote directly from the work of another, use quotation marks. In addition, always include complete information about your source. This information should include author, title, publisher, year of publication, and page numbers.

  Be careful when you put ideas into your own words. It's not just a matter of rearranging the words and choosing synonyms for them. For instance, consider the following passage from *The Language Instinct* by Steven Pinker:

  > Language is a complex, specialized skill, which develops in the child spontaneously, without conscious effort or formal instruction, is deployed without awareness of its underlying logic, is qualitatively the same in every individual, and is distinct from more general abilities to process information or behave intelligently. [1]

  Here's one way of rephrasing the passage, but one that is so close to the original that it amounts to plagiarism:

  > Language is a complicated, specialized ability which develops in the child automatically. Without deliberate energy or teaching, language is engaged in without an understanding of how it works, is distinctly the same for each person, and is separate from more broad skills to integrate data or act cleverly.

A more appropriate rewording of the original passage would be the following, which more clearly rephrases the authors' ideas:

> All individuals share the same basic capacity for language, a capacity that is distinct from other cognitive abilities. While complex, language develops in children regardless of training or even effort on their parts.

Even in this case, it would be wise to cite the source of the facts that you are rephrasing by adding a footnote reference to the original work by Pinker.

The key to avoiding plagiarism to use your own words and, if you use the words, ideas, or thoughts of others, to be sure to cite the source. On the other hand, it is not necessary to have a citation after every sentence. Some ideas are so general ("Children's verbal abilities expand at an astonishing rate") that no source is necessary.

Evaluate: Gold or Pyrite?

After you've accumulated the information that you're seeking, it's important to think critically about the material. You must address several important questions before you can feel confident about what you've found:

- **How authoritative is the information?** You must approach every piece of information you've amassed with a critical eye, trying to determine what the author's biases might be. Clearly, this is no easy task, especially because *they're* the experts and *you're* the beginner. The best approach is to use multiple sources of information and to compare the results. If one source is clearly divergent from the others, then you may reasonably question the reliability of that source.

  Another approach is to consider the publisher of the material. For instance, books published by well-established publishers are carefully reviewed before publication to ensure their accuracy. On the other hand, a book produced by an obscure publishing house may have undergone less scrutiny before publication.

  Be especially critical of information you find on the World Wide Web. It's important to keep in mind that the Web is completely unregulated, and that *anyone* can put *anything* on the Web. Just because a Web site looks attractive and appears to be saying reasonable things, you can't conclude that the information it presents is accurate.

- **How current is the information?** Don't assume that, because you're researching a historically old topic, old sources will suffice. Consider whether what you've found is the most recent and up-to-date approach. Compare older sources to newer ones to identify changes in the ways in which the topic is considered.

- **Is anything missing?** The best way to ensure that you haven't missed anything important is to check out the sources that you have found. Many will have bibliographies and lists of suggested additional readings. By carefully considering this information, you'll be able to get a good sense of the important work in your topic area and to verify that you haven't overlooked some critical source.

Rethink: Putting Information in Context

The information age presents us with great promise and opportunity. Through the use of media such as e-mail and the World Wide Web, we have at our fingertips the ability to communicate with others around the world. We can break the bounds of our physical location and reach across geography to learn about others. The computer keyboard truly can be said to contain "keys"—to the entire earth and its peoples.

At the same time, the world of information can be overwhelming. The amount of information in the world, and the speed at which it enters our lives, can be staggering. It's important, then, to rethink the ways in which we manage information. Specifically, it's essential to consider the following when you deal with any form of information you encounter, whether it's information that you set out to collect or information that you've been exposed to by chance:

- **Consider how the information fits with what you already know**. Information does not enter an empty head; it is added to what you already know about the topic. Ask yourself whether your prior knowledge is affecting the way you view the new information to which you're exposed. Can you look at it objectively? Do you know what your own biases are? Can you open yourself to new information that might contradict your existing beliefs?

- **Identify the assumptions that underlie the information.** Consider the author's perspective when you examine material. Like each of us, every author has a unique way of looking at the world. Think about the author's perspective and consider how it affected the information you're examining. If that perspective were different, how might the information change?

- **Reconsider where you get your information.** Is most of your understanding of what's happening in the world gleaned from television news or short radio newscasts? Consider exposing yourself to other sources. Newspapers, weekly magazines, and news home pages on the World Wide Web all provide coverage of news events.

- **Make time for your yourself.** Finally, don't get so caught up in gathering material for course assignments that you neglect your own needs. Part of the fun of college is exposing yourself to a wide variety of information sources. The library shouldn't just be a place associated with getting assignments done. The Web shouldn't be only something that you use to do research.

WEB P.O.W.E.R.

Basic Computer Skills
1) http://www.citadel.edu/computing/helpdesk/quikg/computstud.html
Computing at the Citadel. This site is maintained by The Citadel (the military college in South Carolina) to help train their students in basic computer skills. It offers a series of study guides for topics related to computing skills. Check out the Help Desk Quick-Menu where you'll find guides to the World Wide Web, Wordperfect 6.1, and much more.

Libraries
2) http://www.ipl.org
"The Internet Public Library". This is the first public library on the internet. Their mission is to discover and organize quality information resources. There are online text collections of over 7,000 titles (a search engine is provided to help you find what your looking for) and guides to periodicals and newspapers.

Web Search Engines
3) http://www.yahoo.com
This is a very popular internet search engine. The search engine is arranged so that you can either search for a specific topic or browse through prearranged categories such as education, health, social science, and more. You can also easily access the latest news headlines and weather forecasts.

4) http://www.psychcrawler.com
Psychcrawler is a search engine supported by the American Psychological Association, created to aid specifically in web searches of current APA materials.

---

[1] Pinker, S. 1995. *The Language Instinct.* New York: Harper-Collins Publishers, Inc., 18.

Chapter 7

Taking Notes

Lucas Mays had been home for the past three weeks with chicken pox. Chicken pox in college! He couldn't believe it. Lucas was hoping to be able to finish out the rest of the semester and most of his professors were pretty understanding, letting him turn in assignments late, but he had missed a lot of classes and wasn't sure that it was really going to be possible to catch up.

His teaching assistant for Abnormal Psych, Karen, was especially helpful, giving him photocopies of her class notes. Her notes were amazing—especially compared to his own! For one thing, he could actually read her writing. Generally, his own notes were a bunch of chicken scratches surrounded by some doodles. Not only were the notes readable, but Karen seemed to actually be able to capture the message that Professor Knight was trying to get across. When Lucas left class each day, his own notes usually consisted of a bunch of random words and definitions, things he often realized later that he could have just gotten from the textbook. Finally, there was actually some organization to her notes. He could tell how the different terms fit together just by reading through her notes. With these notes he felt he actually had a good handle on the material he'd missed—he also felt as though he might be able to take better notes himself from now on.

Looking Ahead

However we learn the lesson, good notetaking abilities can be a lifesaver for our academic careers. Knowing how to take effective notes on class lectures and material we read can help us achieve great academic success.

In this chapter we discuss effective strategies for taking notes in class, during other oral presentations, and from written sources, such as textbooks. You will see that there's a lot more to good notetaking than you probably think—and a lot less, especially if you view notetaking as essentially "getting everything down on paper." As we consider notetaking, we'll pause along the way to discuss the tools of the notetaking trade, how to think your way to good notes, and how to deal with unorganized instructors.

Duly Noted: Taking Effective Class Notes

You know the type: the person who acts as a human tape recorder in class, desperately trying to write down everything the instructor says. No spoken word goes unwritten. And you know what you think to yourself: "If only I could be so industrious, so painstaking in the notes I take, I'd do so much better in my classes."

You're absolutely wrong. The sign of good notetaking is not writing down every word that an instructor utters. In fact, in the case of taking notes, less is often more. We'll see why as we consider the basic steps in P.O.W.E.R. notetaking.

But first, take a look at yourself and consider what type of notetaker you are.

Prepare: Remembering Class Goals

As with other academic activities, preparation for taking notes is critical. The following steps will prepare you for action:

- **Identify the instructor's—and your—goals for the course.** On the first day of class, almost all instructors discuss what they'll be covering over the course of the semester. The information you get during that first session and through the syllabus is critical, because it allows you to calculate the basic direction the instructor plans to take during the course. And even if the instructor's goals aren't stated explicitly, you should attempt to figure them out, either by asking directly or by actively listening to what the instructor has to say and inferring what he or she is trying to achieve. (Refer back to Chapter 2 for active listening techniques.)

  But don't just stop with the instructor's goals for the course. In addition to those "external" goals, you should have your own goals. What is it you wish to learn from the course? What is it you hope to accomplish? How will the information from the course help you to enhance your knowledge, to achieve your dreams, to improve yourself as a person?

  It's important to record these goals by writing them down in a notebook or in some other document. Explicitly stating both your instructor's and your own goals will help you to focus your notetaking on what is important. It will permit you to think actively about the course content and to sharpen your focus on the material being discussed in class.

- **Complete assignments before coming to class.** Always come to class prepared by having done all of your assignments beforehand. Instructors make the assumption that their students have done what they've assigned, and their lectures are based upon that assumption. It's virtually impossible to catch on to the gist of a lecture if you haven't completed the assignments.

- **Accept the instructor, warts and all.** Not every instructor is a great orator or brilliant lecturer. Accept the fact that, just as there are differences in performance between students, some instructors are more adept at lecturing than others.

  Even shortcomings can be turned into opportunities to advance your own agenda. For instance, a repetitious or slow-speaking lecturer can give you time to focus your thinking ("What *is* he trying to say?") and permit you to organize your notes more effectively.

- **Perform a preclass warm up.** No, this doesn't mean that you should be doing jumping jacks just before the class starts. It does mean, however, that you should review your notes from the previous lecture, looking over what the instructor said and where the lecture left off. You should also briefly review the textbook reading and any other material that is germane to the class.

  The warm-up doesn't have to be long. The goal is simply to refresh yourself, to get yourself into the right frame of mind for the class. In the same way that a five-minute warm-up before a run can prevent muscle spasms in your legs, a five-minute mental warm-up can prevent cramped and strained brain muscles.

Organize: Get Your Stuff Together

What kind of writing utensil and paper will work best? There are several considerations. First, using a pen is generally better than using a pencil. Compared to pencil, ink is less likely to smudge, it generally requires less effort to complete the physical act of writing, and what you produce with ink is usually brighter and clearer—and therefore easier to use when studying. On the other hand, for statistics classes, where you may be copying down formulas in class, a pencil might be better, because it's easier to erase if you make a mistake when copying detailed, complex information.

Sometimes you may want to use a combination of pen and pencil. And in some cases you might use several different colors. One color—such as red—might signify important information that the instructor mentions will be on the test. Another color might be reserved for definitions or material that is copied from the board. And a third might be used for notes on what your instructor says.

You also have a choice of many different kinds of notebooks. Loose-leaf notebooks are particularly good because they permit you to go back later and change the order of the pages or add additional material in the appropriate spot. But whatever kind of notebook you use, only use one side of the page for writing; keep one side free of notes. There may be times when you're studying that you'll want to spread out your notes in front of you, and it's much easier if no material is written on the back of the pages.

You should configure notebook pages spatially to optimize later review. According to educator Walter Pauk,[1] the best way to do this is to draw a line down the left side of your notebook page, about 2 ½ inches from the left-hand margin. Keep the notes you write in class to the right of the line. Later, when it comes time to review your notes, you'll be able to jot down a key word, phrase, or major idea on the left side of the page (see following page for an example).

Another question you need to answer is whether to take your textbook to class. Sometimes instructors will refer to information contained in it, and sometimes it's useful to have it handy in order to clarify information that is being discussed. You can also use it to look up key terms that may momentarily escape you. But don't, under any circumstances, use class time as an opportunity to read the textbook!

Finally, if you're quite comfortable with computers and have a laptop, you might want to consider using it to take notes. There are several advantages: Legibility problems are avoided, and it's easy to go back and revise after you've taken the notes. It's also simple to add material later.

	Notes on Memory Tricks of the Trade
	Mnemonics
Roy G. Biv	*acronyms*
Every good boy deserves fun	*acrostics*
30 days hath September	*rhyming*
Unfinished Symphony	*jingles*
room and furniture	*loci technique*
sun, zoo, me, store...	*peg method*
	Using senses
	moving
	draw, diagram
	visualize
	Overlearning

Despite their pluses, laptops also have minuses. For one thing, you may be tempted to take down everything that the instructor says—far more than is optimal, as we'll see next when we discuss the actual process of taking notes. In addition, it's hard to make notes in the margins, copy graphical material that the instructor may present in class, reproduce formulas, or circle key ideas. Furthermore, the clattering of the keyboard may be annoying to your fellow students.

Work: Processing—Not Copying—Information

With pen poised, you're ready to begin the work of notetaking. The instructor begins to speak, and you start to write as quickly as you can, taking down every word you hear.

Stop! You've made your first mistake. If you think that the central act in taking notes is writing, you're wrong. Notetaking involves *listening* and *thinking* far more than writing. To see how this is true, consider the following recommended procedures for taking notes:

- **Listen for the key ideas.** Not every sentence in a lecture is equally important, and one of the most useful skills you can develop is separating the key ideas from supporting information. Good lecturers strive to make just a few main points. The rest of what they say consists of explanation, examples, and other supportive material that expands upon the key ideas.

  Your job, then, is to distinguish the key ideas from those that are of less importance. To do this, you need to be alert and always searching for the meta-message of your instructor's words. As we first discussed in Chapter 2, the **meta-message** consists of the underlying main ideas that a speaker is seeking to convey—the meaning behind the overt message you hear.

How can you discern the meta-message? One way is to listen for key words. Instructors know what's important in their lecture; your job is to figure it out, not from what they say, but from how they say it.

For instance, listen for clues about the importance of material. Phrases like "don't forget…," "be sure to remember that…," "you need to know…," "the most important thing that must be considered…," "there are four problems with this approach…," and—a big one—"this will be on the test…" all should cause you to sit up and take notice.

You should also look for nonverbal signs that indicate the importance of particular material. When instructors pause, raise their eyes, glance at their notes, or otherwise change their demeanor, these behaviors should be a signal that what they're about to say is important.

Another key sign of importance is repetition. If an instructor says the same thing in several ways, it's a clear sign that the material being discussed is critical.

- **Use short, abbreviated phrases—not full sentences.** Forget everything you've ever heard about always writing in full sentences. It simply doesn't apply to notetaking. If you try to write in complete sentences, you'll soon become bogged down. In fact, if you take notes in full sentences, you'll be tempted to try transcribing every word uttered by the instructor, which, as you now know, is not a good idea at all.

  Instead, write in phrases, using only key words or terms. Save full sentences for definitions or quotes that your instructor clearly wants you to know verbatim.

- **Take notes in outline form.** It's often useful to take notes in the form of an outline. It's best to be formal about it, using roman numerals, regular numbers, and capital and small letters. Or, if you prefer, you can also simply use outlining indentations without assigning numbers and letters.

  Outlining serves a number of functions. It forces you to try constantly to determine the structure of the lecture to which you're listening. As we discussed in Chapter 4, material that is organized and linked together is more easily remembered. Outlining also keeps your mind from drifting away from the lecture. The effort involved in seeking out the structure of the lecture will help keep you focused on the material being discussed.

Try It! #1
Outlining a Lecture

Read the following lecture about self-presentation. Outline it as you read. See if you can do your outlining "on the fly" as you read, rather than after you have finished reading the entire lecture. You may even want to ask a friend to read you the lecture as you create your outline.

Self-Presentation

One of the most influential, modern theories of self-presentation is Jones and Pittman's Theory of Strategic Self-Presentation. This theory states that actors try to create specific impressions of themselves in targets or to manage perceptions of themselves in order to elicit particular attributions of their behaviors by the targets. Jones and Pittman identify five classes of self-presentational strategies (ingratiation, self-promotion, exemplification, intimidation, supplication) that are distinguished from one another primarily based upon the particular attribution the actor is seeking to invoke in the target (likability, competence, worthiness, dangerous, helpless).

Jones and his colleagues suggest that ingratiation behaviors are different from other types of self-presentational strategies because ingratiation behaviors tend to be "illicit." By illicit, Jones and Pittman are referring to their belief that ingratiators often conceal their desire to be liked both from themselves, as well as others. If targets are aware of attempts to ingratiate, the tactics can backfire and produce less liking. In addition, individuals attempting to get others to like them may face what Jones and Pittman have labeled the "ingratiator's dilemma." As an individual's dependence on the target increases, the likelihood that ingratiation will succeed decreases. This inverse relationship exists because as an individual becomes more dependent on a target, the ingratiation tactics become more identifiable. Examples of the types of tactics used to ingratiate are conformity, other-enhancement, favor-doing (such as creating a debt by offering to do something for the other person), and self-description.

The second class of self-presentational behaviors are called self-promotional behaviors. To enhance attributions of competence, individuals may use self-promotional techniques in which they claim responsibility for prior positive performances and accomplishments or they may actually demonstrate their superior abilities to targets. On the other hand, self-promoters may discuss a minor area of weakness in order to create an aura of credibility when discussing more important areas of strength. Unfortunately, self-promoters can face a "self-promoter's paradox"; targets of self-promotion realize that it is often the individuals who are least competent who most strongly proclaim their own competence.

The goal of exemplification behaviors is to create attributions of dedication and moral worthiness. These behaviors may function by raising feelings of guilt in the target although these tactics can fail if the actor is perceived as self-righteous. Exemplification often involves tactics such as self-denial and the helping of others.

Intimidation has as its goal that the target fear the actor. Employing threats or anger, the intimidator creates the expectation of negative consequences in the target. While little research has been done in the area of intimidation, Jones and Pittman suggest that intimidation is most likely to be employed in cases of nonvoluntary relationships, when the intimidator has the resources with which to harm the target, when the target cannot "fight back", and when the intimidator is uninterested in evoking more positive attributions from the target.

Finally, supplication may be used by those individuals lacking the resources to use other strategies. Through the use of strategies such as self-deprecation and help-seeking, actors highlight their own weaknesses and dependency in order to create feelings of nurturance in target individuals and invoke a norm of social responsibility. The risk in using these types of tactics is that the target individual may feel no obligation to obey the social norm, thus leaving the actor in an even more vulnerable position.

Write your outline here:

- **Copy information written on the board or projected from overheads.** If your instructor takes the time to write something out to be displayed in class, you should take the time to copy it. Definitions, quotes, phrases, and formulas—if you see them in writing, they're quite likely important enough to include in your notes. In fact, material displayed prominently has "test item" written all over it. You might want to highlight such material in some way in your notes.

- **Use special notetaking techniques for class discussions.** Not every class is structured as a lecture. In fact, the more a class deviates from straight lecturing and includes class discussion, the greater the challenge it poses for notetaking.

  In such situations, the best approach is to take your cue from the course instructor. Often a discussion will begin with the instructor posing a series of questions. Note those questions—they're an important indicator of what the instructor is interested in. Furthermore, watch the instructor's reaction to particular comments and listen to his or her responses. Particularly enthusiastic responses indicate that the instructor thinks the comment is important, and you'll want to highlight it in your notes. It's also useful to register disagreements between members of the class and the instructor.

  Finally, pay particular attention to the points raised by instructors at the end of discussion classes. Instructors often provide a summary of the discussion, which is worthy of inclusion in your notes. In fact, if the instructor does not spontaneously provide a summary at the end of class, a good strategy is to ask him or her to indicate the key points that you should take away from the session.

- **Use special techniques for "problem instructors."** As all of us know from painful experience, not every instructor has learned the importance of structure in lectures. How do you take notes when the instructor is unfocused, rambles on, goes off on tangents, and otherwise does, for lack of a better term, a lousy job?

  The answer is to make the best of a bad situation and adapt your notetaking strategy to it. When you can establish no clear message or logical sequence to the lecture material, you may be unable to take notes in outline form. In such cases, you'll need to focus more on creating a summary of what is being said, rather than trying to tease out its underlying structure. Write short "paragraphs" that focus on the major ideas being presented. Although the paragraphs certainly shouldn't consist of full sentences, they should provide a reasonable condensation of what the instructor said.

  When you're writing in paragraph form, be sure to leave space after each paragraph. By leaving space, you'll make it easier to go back later and restructure the material at a point when its underlying meaning is clearer.

Evaluate: Do the Notes Make Music?

Toward the end of class, take a quick look at your notes. Now's the time—before the class has ended—to evaluate critically what you've written.

Ask yourself these questions: On a basic level, can you read everything you've written? More importantly, do your notes provide a fair representation of what was covered in class? Do they reflect the emphases of the instructor? Are any key points that were discussed not entirely clear? Do you need clarification of any points that the instructor made? Is any follow-up necessary?

Evaluating your notes is a critical part of the notetaking process. You can get a sense of how effective your notetaking has been, and you get the opportunity to remedy any problems that you find in your notes.

By looking over your notes while you're still in class, you have time to ask your instructor for clarification. Or you can wait till the end and then go up to the instructor and raise your question. Most instructors welcome the opportunity to clarify what they've said. Just make sure that you add what they tell you to your notes so you'll be able to refer to them later.

Before you close up your notebook, you still have an important step to complete: rethinking what you've heard. Minutes spent now in reconsideration can save you hours later. The reason: Rethinking consolidates the new information, linking it to and integrating it with knowledge that you already have.

When should you begin the process of rethinking the material in your notes? The sooner, the better. In class, you should have already begun the process, looking over your notes to clarify and evaluate the information in them. But once class is over, you need to review the material more formally. Here's how to do it:

- **Rethink as soon as possible.** As lawyers like to say, time is of the essence! The rethinking phase of notetaking doesn't have to take long; five to ten minutes is usually sufficient. The more critical issue is *when* you do it. The longer you wait before reconsidering your notes, the less effective the process will be.

  Sometimes you'll be able to get in rethinking time just after the class has ended. In any case, don't let the day end without examining your notes. In fact, reconsidering material just before sleep is sometimes thought to be particularly effective.

- **Make rethinking an active process.** When you review your notes, do so with an eye to improving them. If any information is not entirely clear, change the wording in your notes, adding to or amending what's there. If certain words are hard to read, fix them; it won't be any easier to read them the night before a test—in fact, chances are you'll have even more trouble.

  If, on rethinking the material, you just don't understand something, ask your instructor or a friend to clarify it. And when you receive an explanation, add it to your notes so you won't forget it. (You might want to use a different colored pen for additions to your notes, so you'll know they came later.)

- **Take the broad view.** When you rethink your notes, don't think of them only in terms of a single lecture or a single class. Instead, take a longer view. Ask yourself how they fit into the broader themes of the class and the goals that you and the instructor have for the semester. How will the information be useful to you? Why did the instructor emphasize a particular point?

  If you've configured your notes by leaving a 2 ½-inch column on the left-hand side of the page, now is the time to make use of that blank column. Write down key words, significant points, major concepts, controversies, and questions. The process of adding this information will not only help you to rethink the material now, it will also provide guideposts when you study before a test.

- **Create concept maps.** As we've discussed in Chapter 2, concept mapping is a method for structuring written material graphically by grouping and connecting key ideas and themes.

  Building a concept map has several advantages. It forces you to rethink the material in your notes in a new style—particularly important if you used traditional outlining while taking the notes. In addition, it helps you to tie together the material for a given class session. Finally, it will help you to a build a master concept map later, when you're studying the material for a final exam.

Try It! #2
Practice Your Notetaking Skills

Practice your notetaking skills, using any techniques you find helpful, by listening to an extended oral presentation and taking notes.

The kind of extended presentation you should look for may be a radio or television news story (not the "sound bite" type, but an extended piece such as is found on public radio or television), a speech (if the timing is right, the president's annual State of the Union speech in January or a similar public address is ideal), or a recording of a historical speech (such as one of President Roosevelt's inaugural addresses or fireside chats, a speech by John F. Kennedy or Ronald Reagan, an address by Martin Luther King, Jr., or a similar political speech).

After you have taken notes, use the techniques discussed in this chapter to evaluate and rethink them. Creating a concept map may be particularly helpful.

Duly Noted, Part 2: Taking Effective Notes from the Written Word

Weighing as much as five pounds, bulky and awkward, and filled with more information than you think anyone could ever need to know, it's the meat-and-potatoes of college life: your course textbook. You might feel intimidated by its size; you might feel annoyed at its cost; you might feel you'll never be able to read it, let alone understand, learn, and recall the material in it. How will you manage?

The answer is found in the principles we've already discussed. By combining the reading skills we discussed in Chapter 2 and the notetaking skills we've been going over in this chapter, you'll be able to meet the challenge that textbooks present.

However, certain aspects of taking notes from textbooks are unique. Before considering them below, it's important to make a distinction between two different kinds of notes that are derived from reading: study notes and research notes.

Study notes are notes taken for the purpose of reviewing material. They are the kind of notes that you take in class to study from later. **Research notes**, in contrast, are notes that you take to write a paper or prepare a report.

Because we considered procedures for taking research notes in Chapter 6, we'll focus on study notes here. What's the best approach to taking study notes from written material, such as magazines, books, journals, and encyclopedias? Several strategies are useful. Which approach works best depends on whether you're able to write on the material you wish to take notes on.

Material you own and can write on. When the material you wish to take notes on belongs to you, your task is both simpler and more complex. It's simpler because you can write on it, and consequently you're free to annotate the text directly by underlining or writing in the margins. On the other hand, it's more complex because it may not be clear what should go in your text notes. Here are some suggestions:

- **Integrate your text notes into your study notes.** If you wish to create study notes from written material that you can write text notes on, start by annotating the pages as you normally would. Use the techniques that have worked best for you: highlighting, underlining, circling, marginal notes—whatever you generally use. (You might want to review the sections in Chapter 2 that discuss what you should be writing while you're reading.)

    Later, after you've finished reading and annotating the material, it's time to create study notes. While it's still fresh in your mind, go back over the material and your text annotations, and create your study notes.

The study notes should provide a summary of the key points. They might be in outline form, or in the form of concept maps. Whatever their form, they should supplement and summarize the annotations you've made on the printed page. The greater the difference between what's on the printed page and what's in your study notes, the better, in terms of later recalling the information and actually using the notes for studying.

Furthermore, any notes you take should stand on their own. For instance, they should include enough information to be useful whether or not the printed material is available.

- **Use flash cards.** If you feel confident that the annotations you've written in the book are sufficiently comprehensive, you might consider taking notes on flash cards. **Flash cards** are simply 3" x 5" note cards that contain key pieces of information that you need to remember. One of the greatest virtues of flash cards is their portability. Because they are small, they can fit into your pocket or handbag, and you can look at them at odd times when you have a spare moment.

Material you can't write on. Taking notes on material that can't be written on is a different story. Library books, magazine, journal articles, and material on library reserve that are shared with others require a different approach. The following suggestions apply in such cases:

- **Approach the written material as you would a class lecture.** The techniques we discussed earlier for taking notes in class can all be adapted for taking notes from written material. In fact, the task is often easier, because, as is not the case with the spoken word, you'll be able to refer back to what was said earlier—it's in black-and-white in front of you.

  Use all the tricks of the trade we discussed earlier for taking notes from a class lecture. Look for the key ideas, definitions, quotes, and formulas and include them in your notes. Use the headings that are included in the text, such as chapter and section titles. Bold or italic type is also a clue that an important point is being made. Graphs and charts often provide critical information.

  What kind of notes should you take? It's largely up to you. Use the same form of notetaking that you use in class lectures. If the material is critical, though, you might want to consider a more aggressive form of notetaking: creating a summary of the information, as we consider next.

- **Write a précis.** Writing a **précis** (pronounced "PRAY-see" or "pray-SEE")—a summary of a longer document—is often an excellent way of capturing the content of material you'll wish to study later. In French, précis means both "precise" and "concise," and that should be your goal: producing an accurate, yet condensed, version of a longer work.

  Creating a précis is effective for several reasons. One is that the act of writing a précis necessitates that you analyze what is most important in the material you're reading. You need to strip away information that is not directly relevant to the main thrust of the material and focus only on what is most important. Doing so will clarify what is—and isn't—critical. Furthermore, writing a précis provides you with a document that will be an invaluable study aid, especially because you may have had to return the original material to the library and won't have it when you need to study it.

  To create a précis, identify the main ideas and concepts of the material you're reading. Consider the point the author is trying to make and the evidence that is presented in support of that point. Try to determine what is most important and what is of only secondary importance in the material. In addition, take a critical look at the information and note any weaknesses in the author's arguments. Seek to identify any material that's not included that would have strengthened the author's contentions.

  Finally, write the précis. Remember that your goal is to create a short document that captures the strengths of the original material. Begin with a topic sentence that conveys the main point, and then provide support for that point. Refer to supportive evidence that the author provides—or doesn't but should have. Remember that your goal is to make a document that stands on its own, one that will refresh your memory of the original material when it comes time to study.

Because writing a précis is time-consuming, you'll probably want to write one only when the material you're summarizing is important and you won't have access to it in the future. In such cases, a précis can be an invaluable study tool.

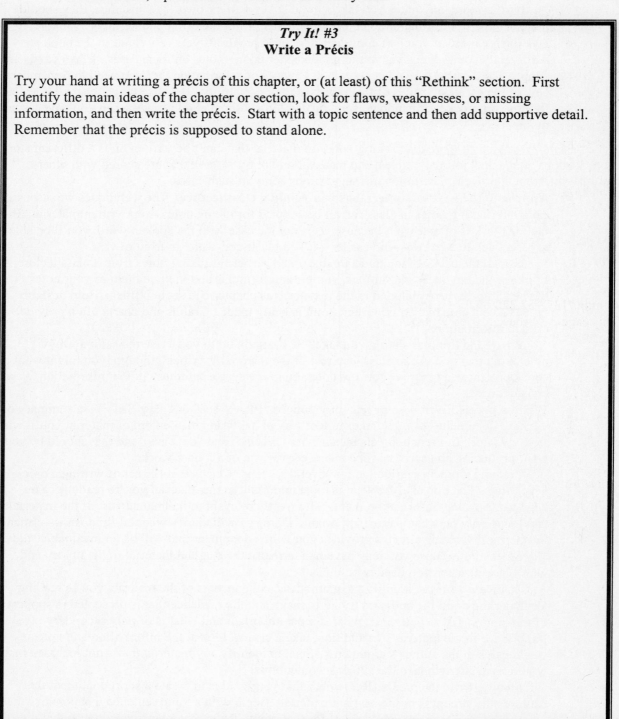

Try It! #3
Write a Précis

Try your hand at writing a précis of this chapter, or (at least) of this "Rethink" section. First identify the main ideas of the chapter or section, look for flaws, weaknesses, or missing information, and then write the précis. Start with a topic sentence and then add supportive detail. Remember that the précis is supposed to stand alone.

WEB P.O.W.E.R.

Cornell Notetaking System
1) www.whc.net/irish/note.htm
The Cornell Notetaking System can help students who want to improve the organization of their notes. One strength of this system is that it allows you to make use of your existing strengths as a notetaker. This means that learning the system requires a minimum of preparation and adjustment. This page describes how the system works.

Organizing Information into Tables
2) http://www.coun.uvic.ca/learn/program/hndouts/class5.html
It is often helpful to organize the information you have to learn into table form. This site gives two examples in which information is presented as passages and then organized into table form. The site allows you to try organizing the information into table form yourself before finding out how the authors have organized their table. This is a great way to get some practice at organizing tables of information.

Learning to use a Concept Map
3) http://www.coun.uvic.ca/learn/program/hndouts/class1.html
Another effective method for organizing complicated information is in the form of a concept map. This site is another tutorial site that presents information in a passage and then asks you to create your own concept map. The concept map created by the authors is only a click away.

Basic Notetaking Skills
4) http://137.132.225.6/UFM/effect/Es4_3_3.html
This page describes a variety of effective notetaking skills, including how to organize your notes, how to use abbreviations, and how to improve the visual impact of your notes. An example of concept mapping is also described.

Learning in Lecture
5) http://137.132.225.6/UFM/effect/Es4_1_1.html
This page addresses how to effectively learn material presented in lecture. The purpose of a lecture is described and several helpful hints for figuring out what lecture information is most important are explained.

---

[1] Pauk, W. 1974. *How to Study in College.* Boston: Houghton Mifflin.

Chapter 8

Taking Tests

"You've got to be kidding me," thought Leila. "How can I possibly learn five chapters of material for one exam?"

Coming from a small high school with a graduating class of just 60 students, Leila Bolger was pretty overwhelmed by life at the university. She was used to talking one-to-one with her teachers in each of her classes. One of the hardest things to get used to was the size of the classes. Her Introductory Psychology class was over 300 students.

But it wasn't just the size of the class, it was the way the professors tested students. She understood *why* the professor gave multiple choice exams—there were just too many students to be able to grade that many essay exams, but the only time she'd taken a multiple choice exam was for the SAT. "I know what types of questions teachers ask on essay exams, but how can I possibly prepare for a test containing 50 multiple choice questions when it covers so much material?"

Looking Ahead

For many psychology students, tests represent the most anxiety-producing events in their college careers. They needn't be. There are strategies and techniques you can learn to reduce the fearsomeness of tests. In fact, in some ways learning *how* to take tests is as important as learning the content that they cover. Taking tests effectively is an acquired skill. It does not just involve mastering a body of information; it also requires mastering specific test-taking skills.

We consider the nuts and bolts of test-taking in this chapter. We begin by demystifying tests, driving home the point that test performance does not equate to life performance or individual self-worth. We describe the types of tests that you are likely to encounter and recommend some useful preparation strategies that you can apply before you even see a test. We discuss the different types of test questions that are commonly used, and we describe a strategy for test preparation that matches each type.

We continue with a discussion of ways to "tool up" for testing by getting your head and your actual tools, such as pencils and erasers, ready for the event. Then we move into the actual work of testing—sitting down and working through the questions. We discuss several strategies and hints for doing well on a test—and on the different types of test questions.

Prepare: Planning for the Inevitable

Although tests are a fact of academic life, no one on either the giving or receiving end likes certain aspects of them very much.

Students hate tests because they produce fear, anxiety, apprehension about being evaluated, and a focus on grades instead of learning for learning's sake. Instructors hate tests because they produce fear, anxiety, apprehension about being evaluated, and a focus on grades instead of learning for learning's sake. That's right: Students and instructors dislike tests for the very same reasons.

In My Own Words
How I Feel About Tests

What feelings do you have about tests?

What experiences have you had that explain your feelings?

What uses do you think tests serve?

Do you think tests are ever misused? In what ways?

Have you ever learned anything about yourself from a test that you didn't know before?

Do you think your teachers have ever learned anything about you from a test that they didn't know before?

Do you think tests increase fairness or decrease it? Why?

What makes a good test? What characteristics does a good test have?

What makes a bad test? What characteristics does a bad test have?

Have you experienced more good tests or bad tests in your life?

Tests are tools; they are indirect and imperfect measures of what we know. Someone with a great deal of knowledge can do poorly on a test; perhaps his nerves made him blank out completely. Another person can do well on a test despite knowing comparatively little; she may either be lucky or she may have learned some test-taking skills along the way. Both results are essentially flukes, so we should avoid giving the tests that produced the results a power they don't have.

On the other hand, tests can be helpful and they aren't always inaccurate. In fact, there are important reasons why we should welcome the use of tests, for they produce some clear benefits. Consider these:

- Tests tell us what we know.

- Tests show us where there are gaps in our knowledge.

- Tests suggest how we can do better in the future.

- Tests indicate if we've done our best.

- Tests can teach us—about the subject matter, and about ourselves.

How much we reap the benefits of a test depends on a number of considerations: the subject matter involved and how well we prepare for it. Let's take a look at several factors involved in preparing for this inevitable feature of academic life.

- **Everything you do is preparation for tests.** Completing a reading assignment. Writing a paper. Filling out a worksheet.

    Everything—everything—you do during a course helps to prepare you for a test. There is no surer way to get good grades on tests than to attend class faithfully and to complete all class assignments seriously and on time.

- **Know the enemy.** Determine as much as you can about the test before you begin to prepare for it. The more you know about a test, the better you'll be able to get ready.

    To find out about an upcoming test, ask these questions:

    - What material will the test cover?

    - How many questions will be on it?

    - How much time is it expected to take? A full class period? Only part of a period?

    - What kinds of questions will be on the test?

    - How will it be graded?

    - Will sample questions be provided?

    - Are tests from previous terms available?

- **Form a study group. Study groups** are small, informal groups of students whose purpose is to help members work together and study for a test. Some study groups are formed for particular tests, while others meet consistently throughout the term.

    Study groups can be extremely powerful tools because they help accomplish several things. One benefit is that they help members to organize and structure the material, which forces members to approach the material in a logical way. Membership in a study group also helps prevent students from overlooking any potentially important information, either about the test itself or the material on which they're being tested.

    Further, study groups force their members to rework the course material, explaining it in words that they and the other group members will understand. This act of processing information contributes enormously to the members' understanding of the material, and even facilitates recall of the information when it is needed—on the test.

Finally, study groups help motivate members to do their best. When you're part of a study group, you're no longer working just for yourself; your studying also benefits the other study-group members. Not wanting to let down your classmates in a study group may sometimes give more of a push to your study habits than you get from working only for yourself.

- **Match test preparation to question types.** Test questions come in different types, and each requires a somewhat different style of preparation. Let's consider each one in turn.
  - ❑ **Essay questions.** <u>Essay questions</u> require the creation of a fairly extended, on-the-spot composition, written in expository (e.g., explanatory, descriptive, or narrative) form, about some topic.

    Whatever their length, essay exams require that you have a broad knowledge of the material being tested. You'll need to know not just a series of facts, but also the connections between the facts and the ways in which they can be organized logically. The ways in which the various pieces of information on a topic fit together is a key focus of essay exams.

    The best approach to studying for an essay exam involves four steps. This approach assumes that your notes are in the form that we discussed in the previous chapter, with a left-hand column that contains key words, phrases, and questions.

    1. Carefully read your class notes and any notes you've made on assigned readings that will be covered on the upcoming exam. Also go through the readings themselves, reviewing underlined or highlighted material and marginal notes.
    2. Play professor: Think of likely exam questions. To do this, you can use the key words, phrases, concepts, and questions you've earlier created in your notes. In addition, your class instructor may have given you a list of possible essay topics. Whatever you use, write the questions down to make the task concrete.

Try It! #1
Create an Essay Test

Read the following textbook passage about women in the U.S. workforce. Then write at least two essay questions based on the passage, focusing on the relevance of the material to psychological issues.

Women's participation in the paid labor force of the United States has been increasing steadily throughout the twentieth century. No longer is the adult woman associated solely with the role of homemaker. Instead, millions of women—married women and single women, with and without children—are working outside the home. In 1994, more than 59 percent of adult women in the United States held jobs outside the home, as compared with 38 percent in 1960. Thus, a majority of women are now members of the paid labor force, not full-time homemakers.

Yet women entering the job market find their options restricted in important ways. Particularly damaging to women workers is occupation segregation, or confinement to sex-typed "women's jobs." For example, in 1994 women accounted for 98 percent of all secretaries, 96 percent of all private household workers, and 94 percent of all registered nurses. Entering such sex-typed occupations places women in "service" roles which parallel the traditional gender-role standard under which housewives "serve" their husbands.[1]

95

3. Without looking at your notes or your readings, answer each potential essay question—aloud. Don't feel embarrassed about doing this. Talking aloud is far more useful than answering the question silently in your head, and it will better show you where your strengths and weaknesses lie.

4. After you've answered the questions, check yourself by looking at the notes and readings once again. If you feel confident that you've answered particular questions adequately, check them off. You can go back later for a quick review.
    But if there are questions that you had trouble with it, review that material immediately. Reread information about which you don't feel fully confident. Then repeat the third step above, answering the questions again. Eventually you'll reach a level of mastery and assurance about the material, permitting you to take the upcoming essay exam with confidence.

❑   **Multiple-choice, true–false, and matching questions.** **<u>Multiple-choice questions</u>** typically contain a question or statement, followed by a number (usually 4 or 5) of response choices. Your task is to choose the correct response from the possible response choices that are offered.

    <u>True–false questions</u> typically present statements about a topic that are either accurate or inaccurate. Your task is to indicate whether each statement is accurate (true) or inaccurate (false).

    <u>Matching questions</u> usually present two lists of related information, arranged in column form, that examinees must link. Your task is typically to pair terms, concepts, and definitions with one another.

    Almost anything is fair game for multiple-choice, true-false, and matching questions, and so you can't afford to overlook anything when studying. This means that your studying needs to be detail-oriented. And it means that you must put your memory into high gear and master a great many facts.

    As a practical matter, learning a large body of information requires the use of the full battery of memory techniques that we discussed in Chapter 4. It's a particularly good idea to write down important facts on 3" x 5" cards. Remember the advantages of these cards: They're portable and available all the time, and the act of creating them helps drive the material into your memory. Furthermore, you can shuffle them and test yourself repeatedly until you know you've mastered the material.

❑   **Short-answer and fill-in questions.** Short-answer and fill-in questions lie somewhere between essay questions, on the one hand, and multiple-choice, true–false, and matching questions, on the other. **<u>Short-answer questions</u>** require brief responses (at most a few sentences) in a kind of mini-essay. **<u>Fill-in questions</u>** require you to add one or more missing words to a sentence or series of sentences.

    Short-answer and fill-in questions are similar to essays in that they require you to recall key pieces of information; that is, you have to dredge the information up from your memory rather than finding it on the page in front of you, as is the case with multiple-choice, true–false, and matching questions. However, short-answer and fill-in questions—unlike essay questions—typically don't demand that you integrate or compare different types of information. Consequently, the focus of your study should be on the recall of specific, detailed information.

•   **Test yourself.** Once you feel you've mastered the material, test yourself on it. There are several ways to do this. One is to create a complete test for yourself, in writing, making its form as close as possible to what you expect the actual test to be. For instance, if your instructor has told you the classroom test will be primarily made up of short-answer questions, your test should be too. One bonus: Constructing a test is actually an excellent way of studying the material and cementing it into memory.

You might also construct a test and administer it to a classmate or a member of your study group. In turn, you could take a test that someone else has constructed. The combined experience of making and taking a test on the same general subject matter is among the very best ways to prepare for the real thing.

Organize: Mapping Out Your Line of Attack

You've studied a lot, and you're happy with your level of mastery. Or perhaps you have the nagging feeling that there's something you haven't quite gotten to. Or maybe you know you haven't had enough time to study as much as you'd like, and you're expecting a disaster.

Whatever your frame of mind, it will help to organize your plan of attack on the day of the test. What's included on the test is out of your control, but what you bring to it you can control.

For starters, bring the right tools to the test. Have at least two pens and two pencils with you. It's usually best to write in pen because, in general, writing tends to be easier to read in pen than pencil. Having a second pen helps in case the first runs out of ink. But you also might want to have pencils at the ready. Sometimes instructors will use machine-scorable tests, which require the use of pencil. Or there may be test questions that involve computations, and solving them may entail frequent reworking of calculations. Pencils—with erasers—work best in such instances.

You should also be sure to bring a watch to the test, even if there will be a clock on the wall of the classroom. You will want to be able to pace yourself properly during the test. If the classroom clock is not working for some reason, you don't want to be left out in the cold.

Sometimes instructors permit you to use notes and books during the test. If you haven't brought them with you, they're not going to be of much help. So make sure you take them to the exam. Even for closed-book tests, having such material available before the test actually starts may allow you a few minutes of review after you arrive in the classroom.

When you arrive in class on the day of a test, avoid the temptation to compare notes with your friends about how much they've studied. Yes, you might end up feeling good because many of your fellow classmates studied less than you. But chances are that you'll find others who have spent significantly *more* time studying than you—information that will do little to encourage you, and which is likely to be inaccurate in the first place. People often exaggerate or minimize the amount they say they've studied. For instance, statements such as "I was up the last three nights studying" or "I never cracked a book" are probably both inaccurate.

You should also work out a strategy to ready yourself at the starting gate. One way to do this is to plan on panicking. Although it sounds like the worst possible approach, permitting yourself the option of spending a minute feeling panicky will help you to recover from your initial fears.

Finally, listen carefully to what an instructor says before the test is handed out. The instructor may impart some crucial information about what's on the test or inform you of a typographical error on the test. Whatever the instructor says just before the test, you can be sure it's information that you don't want to ignore.

Work: Attack the Test

Take a deep breath—literally.

There's no better way to start work on a test than by taking a deep breath, followed by several others, accompanied by images of success. The deep breaths will help you to overcome any initial panic and anxiety you may be experiencing.

Once you've moved beyond the panic stage, read the test instructions and then skim through the entire exam. Look at the kinds of questions that are asked and pay attention to the way they will be scored. If the point weighting of the various parts of the exam is not clear, ask the instructor to clarify it. Your goal is to know how to allocate your time. You don't want to spend 90 percent of your time on an essay that's worth only 10 percent of the points, and you want to be sure to leave time at the end of the test to check your answers. An initial read-through also helps you verify that you have every page of the exam and that there is no other physical problem with it, such as badly copied pages or ink marks that partially obscure some of the questions.

If there are any lists, formulas, or other key facts that you're concerned you may forget, jot them down now on the back of a test page or on a piece of scrap paper. You may want to refer to this material later during the test.

Once this background work is out of the way, you'll be ready to proceed to actually answering the questions. These principles will help you to do your best on the test:

- **Answer the easiest questions first.** By initially getting the questions out of the way that are easiest, you accomplish several important things. First, you'll be able to get through them relatively quickly, and you'll be leaving yourself more time to think about the tougher questions later. In addition, moving through a series of questions without a struggle will build your confidence. Finally, working through a number of questions will build up a base of points that may be enough to earn you at least a minimally acceptable grade. Both realistically and psychologically, after you complete the easier items, everything else you do will amount to bringing you closer to an "A."

- **Write legibly on one side of the paper.** If an instructor can't read what you've written, you're not going to get credit for it, no matter how brilliant your answer. So be sure to keep your handwriting legible.

    It's also a good idea to write your answers to essay questions on only one side of a page. This will allow you to go back later and add or revise information. (If you do this, be sure to indicate by a note on your answer sheets that there's material on the back sides of the pages so that your instructor won't overlook part of your answers.)

- **Master machine-scored tests.** Tests will sometimes be scored, in part, by computer. In such cases, you'll usually have to indicate your answers by filling in with a pencil circles or squares on a computer answer sheet.

    Be careful! A stray mark or smudge can cause the computer scanner to misread your answer sheet, producing errors in grading. Be sure to bring a good eraser in addition to a pencil; the biggest source of mistakes in machine grading is incomplete erasing on a test.

    Also be careful if, in answering the easiest questions first, you skip one or more questions. Whenever you skip a question, be sure to skip also the row of answer circles on the answer sheet that corresponds to it, or all your answers will be off by one.

    It's best to write your answers not only on the answer sheet but also on the test itself. That way you can go back and check your answers easily—a step you should take frequently.

- **Tailor test-taking strategies to the different types of items.** Every type of item requires a particular approach. Use these strategies to tailor your strategy to specific kinds of questions:
    - ❑ **Essay questions.** Essay questions, with their emphasis on description and analysis, often present challenges because they are relatively unstructured. Unless you're careful, it's easy to wander off and begin to answer questions that were never asked. To prevent that problem, the first thing to do is read the question carefully, noting what specifically is being asked. If your essay will be lengthy, you might even want to write a short outline.

        Pay attention to key words that indicate what, specifically, the instructor is looking for in an answer. As you can see in Table 8-1, certain action words are commonly used in essays, and you should understand them fully. For instance, knowing the distinction between "compare" and "contrast" can spell the difference between success and failure.

Table 8-1

Action Words for Essays

These words are commonly used in essay questions. Learning the distinctions between them will help you during tests.

Analyze: Examine and break into component parts
Compare: Describe similarities and differences.
Contrast: Explain and distinguish differences.
Compare and contrast: Describe and explain similarities and differences.
Define: Provide the meaning
Discuss: Explain, review, and consider
Explain: Clarify, justify, and illustrate
Enumerate: Provide a listing of ideas, concepts, reasons, items, etc.
Evaluate: Provide pros and cons of something; provide an opinion, and justify it
Explain: Give reasons why or how; provide a series of steps; show how things fit together
Illustrate: Provide examples; show instances
Interpret: Explain or translate the meaning of something
Outline: Provide a framework or explanation—usually in narrative form—of a concept, idea, event, or
    phenomenon.
Prove: Using evidence and arguments, convince the reader about something
Relate: Show how things fit together; provide analogies
State: Assert or explain
Summarize: Provide a condensed, precise list or narrative
Trace: Track or sketch out how events or circumstances have evolved; provide a history or timeline

Be brief and to the point in your essay. Avoid flowery introductory language. The sentence "In our study of the principles of learning, it may be useful to ponder how the work of Ivan Pavlov came to represent such an important milestone in the field, and it will be seen that there are several critical reasons why it did have such an impact" could be stated far more economically as "The work of Ivan Pavlov is important for several reasons."

Essays are improved when they include examples and point out differences. Your response should follow a logical sequence, and—above all—it should address every aspect of the question that it addresses. Because essays often contain several different, embedded questions, you have to be certain that you have answered every part.

❑ **Multiple-choice questions.** If you've ever looked at a multiple-choice question and said to yourself, "Every choice seems right," you know that this type of question presents a special challenge. Yet there are strategies that can help you deal with multiple-choice questions.

First, read the instructions carefully to determine whether only one response choice will be correct, or whether more than one of the choices may be correct. Almost always only one choice is right, but in some cases it may be possible for several choices to be correct.

Turn to the first question and read the question part—the part before the response choices. Before you look at the choices, try to answer the question in your head. This can help you avoid being confused by inappropriate choices.

Next, carefully read through every choice. Even if you come to one that you think is right, keep reading—there may be a subsequent answer that is better.

Look for certain key qualifier words, such as absolutes like "every," "always," "only," "none," and "never." As explained below, choices that contain such absolute words are rarely correct. On the other hand, less absolute words, such as "generally," "usually," "often," "rarely," "seldom," and "typically" may indicate a correct response.

Be especially on guard for the word "not," which negates the sentence ("The one key concept that is *not* involved in classical conditioning is…"). It's easy to gloss over "not," and if you have the misfortune to do so, it will be nearly impossible to answer the item correctly.

If you're having trouble understanding a question, underline key words or phrases, or try to break the question into different short sections.

Finally, use an **educated guessing** strategy—which is very different from wild or random guessing. Unless you are penalized for wrong answers (a scoring rule by which wrong answers are deducted from the points you have earned on other questions, rather than merely not counting at all toward your score), it always pays to guess.

The first step in educated guessing is to eliminate any obviously false answers. This immediately increases the odds of your answering correctly.

The next step is to examine the remaining choices closely. Does one choice include a qualifier that makes it unlikely ("rapid eye movements (REM) can always be seen during sleep")? Does one choice include a subtle factual error? In such cases, you may be able to ferret out the correct response by eliminating the others.

But what if you have absolutely no idea which is the right response? There are some last resort principles. One is that—all other things being equal—an answer that says "all of the above" is slightly more likely to be correct than not. A second last resort principle is that the broader and more inclusive an answer, the more likely it is to be correct. Remember, though: These are principles of last resort, not universals. Don't apply them routinely.

❑ **True–false questions.** Although most of the principles we've already discussed apply equally well to true–false questions, a few additional tricks of the trade may help you with this question type.

Begin a set of true–false questions by marking all the items you're sure are correct. But don't rush; it's more important than ever to read every part of a true–false question, because key words such as "never," "always," and "sometimes" often determine the appropriate response.

If you don't have a clue about whether a statement is true or false, here's another last resort principle: choose true. In general, more statements on a true–false test are likely to be true than false.

❑ **Matching questions.** Matching questions typically present you with two columns of related information, which you must link using a process of elimination. For example, a list of terms or concepts may be presented in one column, along with a list of corresponding definitions or explanations in the second column. The best strategy is to reduce the size of both columns by matching the items you're most confident about first; this will leave a short list in each column, and the final matching may become apparent.

❑ **Short-answer and fill-in questions.** Short-answer and essay questions require a different level of response from multiple-choice, true–false, and matching questions. While the others test the ability to *recognize and select* a correct response, short-answer and fill-in questions test at a deeper level, closer to what is called for in an essay.

Short-answer and fill-in questions basically require you to *generate and supply* specific information in your own words. Unlike essays, which are more free-form and may have several possible answers, short-answer and fill-in questions are quite specific.

There is usually only one answer, which you must come up with on your own. Responding to them, then, requires that you pay special attention to what, in particular, you are being asked.

Use both the instructions for the questions and the questions themselves to determine the level of specificity that is needed in an answer. Furthermore—in addition to giving the correct answer—try not to provide too much or too little information. Usually, brevity is best.

Evaluate: Your Final Examination

The last few minutes of a test are like the final moments of a marathon. You need to muster your energy and put an extra kick in your step. It can be make-or-break time.

Start evaluating your test by looking for obvious mistakes. Make sure you've answered every question and haven't skipped any parts of questions. If there is a separate answer sheet, check to see that all your answers have been recorded on the answer sheet and in the right spot.

If the test has included essay and short-answer questions, proofread your responses. Check for obvious errors—misspellings, missing words, and repetitions. Make sure you've responded to every part of each question, and that each essay, as a whole, makes sense. You won't have time to rewrite your essay if you're dissatisfied with it, but you may be able to add a few ideas or transitions that will make it hold together better.

The final evaluation should also encompass your responses to multiple-choice, true–false, and matching questions. If there are some items that you haven't yet answered because you couldn't remember the necessary information, now's the time to take stab at them. Guess randomly if you must, but answer them—so long as there's no "guessing penalty."

What about items that you initially were genuinely unsure about, and you guessed at the answer? Unless you have a good reason to change your original answer—such as a new insight or a sudden recollection of some key information—your first guess is likely your best guess.

After evaluating and checking your answers, you may reach a point when there is still some time left. What to do? If you're satisfied with your responses, it's simply time to tell yourself, "*Let it go.*"

"Disaster! I've run out of time!" It's a nightmarish feeling: The clock is ticking relentlessly, and it's clear that you don't have enough time to finish the test. What should you do?

Stop work! Although this advice may sound foolish, in fact the most important thing to do is to take a minute to calm yourself. Take some deep breaths to replace the feelings of panic that are likely welling up inside you. Collect your thoughts, and plan a strategy for the last moments of the test.

If there are essays that remain undone, consider how you'd answer them if you had more time. Then write an outline of each answer. If you don't have time even for that, write a key few words. Writing something is better than handing in a blank page, and you may get at least some credit for your response. The key principle here: Something is better than nothing, and even one point is worth more than no points.

The same principle holds for other types of questions. Even wild guesses are almost always better than not responding at all to an item. So rather than telling yourself you've certainly failed and giving up, do as much as you can in the remaining moments of the exam period.

Rethink: The Real Test of Learning

A week has gone by since you took the test, and your instructor is about to hand the graded exams back. All sorts of thoughts run through your head. "How did I do?" "Did I perform as well as my classmates?" "Will I be pleased with my results?" "Will the results reflect the amount of effort I put into studying?" "Will I be embarrassed by my grade?"

Most of us focus on the evaluative aspects of tests. We look at the grade we've received on a test and take it to be a measure of something important. It's a natural reaction.

But there's another way to look at test results: They can help guide us toward future success. By looking at what we've learned (and haven't learned) about a given subject, we'll be in a better position to know what to focus on when we take future exams. Furthermore, by examining the kinds of mistakes we make, it's more likely that we can do better in the future.

Consequently, when you receive a test back, it's a signal to rethink what you've learned and consider your performance. Begin by looking at your mistakes. Did you misunderstand or misapply some principle? Was there a certain aspect of the material covered on the test that you missed? Were there particular kinds of information that you didn't know you needed to know?

Once you have a good idea of what material you didn't fully understand or remember, write down a summary of this information. In order to do this, make sure you get the correct answers to the items you missed—from your instructor, fellow classmates, or a book. If it's a math exam, rework problems you've missed. Finally, summarize—in writing—the material you had trouble with. This will help you study for future exams that cover the same material.

Try It! #2

Rethink a Recent Test

Read over a recent test that was graded and returned by an instructor. Read the comments the instructor made on the test, and consider your performance on each question. Then answer these questions.

What does the test reveal about your knowledge of the subject? What do you know about the subject? What do you not yet know?

What kinds of mistakes did you make? Were your mistakes mostly factual? Do they reveal a misunderstanding of principles or concepts?

Did you tend to make the same kind of mistake repeatedly?

What sorts of responses did the instructor especially like?

Did you use effective test-taking skills on the test? If you didn't, which aspects of test-taking require improvement: preparation for testing, organization before the test, the actual work of answering questions during the test, or the evaluation of your work at the end of the test session?

What would you do the same next time, and what would you do differently?

After you have a good sense of which material you missed, rethink your test-taking techniques. Did you lose points because of your test-taking skills? Did you make careless errors, such as forgetting to fill in a question or misreading the directions? Was your handwriting so sloppy that your instructor couldn't read it? Use this information as a guidepost for future improvement.

Finally, if you're dissatisfied with your performance, talk to your instructor—not to complain, but to seek help. Instructors don't like to give bad grades, and they may be able to point out problems in your test that you can address readily so you can do better in the future. Demonstrate to your instructor that you want to do better and are willing to put in the work to get there. The worst thing to do is rip up the test and skulk out of the class in embarrassment. Remember, you're not the first person to get a bad grade, and the power to improve your test-taking performance lies within you.

WEB P.O.W.E.R.

Tactics for Managing Stress and Anxiety
1) http://www.coun.uvic.ca/personal/stress/html
This site offers several suggestions that you might find very helpful in managing and reducing your level of stress and anxiety. The techniques may help you deal with test-related anxiety, as well as academic-related anxiety in general. Not all of the techniques work for everyone. Try them and use the ones that work best for you.

Multiple-Choice Exams
2) http://www.coun.uvic.ca/learn/program/handouts/multicho.html
This page offers some valuable suggestions about how to approach multiple-choice exams. Several types of multiple-choice questions are described and strategies for multiple-choice questions are explained. There are helpful hints about what to look for in the wording of both the questions and the answer choices in a multiple-choice exam.

Essay Questions
3) http://www.coun.uvic.ca/learn/program/handouts/simple.html
This page gives examples of question words that are often to be found in essay assignments or in essay questions on exams. Possible "plans of action" for each of the question types are outlined. These outlines can be useful as a starting point for understanding how to approach effectively answering essay questions.

Open-Book Exams
4) http://137.132.225.6/UFM/effect/Es4_3_4.html
This page is maintained by the The National University of Singapore and is aimed at helping it's students prepare for open-book exams. The site explains the rationale, logistics, and expectations behind an open-book exam so that you can prepare yourself appropriately.

---

[1] Schaefer, R.T., & Lamm, R.P. 1998. *Sociology*. New York: McGraw-Hill, 335.

Key Terms and Concepts

ABBCC structure: The structure of the typical research paper, consisting of argument, background, body, counterarguments, and conclusion

Abstract: A short summary of the contents of a journal article

Acronym: A word or phrase formed by the first letters of a series of terms

Acrostic: A sentence in which the first letters of the words correspond to material that is to be remembered

Advance organizers: Broad, general ideas related to material that is to be read or heard, which pave the way for subsequent learning

Attention span: The length of time that attention is typically sustained

Brainstorming: A technique for generating ideas by saying out loud as many ideas as can be thought of in a fixed period of time

Browser: A program that provides a way of navigating around the information on the World Wide Web

Call number: A unique classification number assigned to every book (or other resource) in a library, which provides a key to locating it

Concept mapping: A method of structuring written material by graphically grouping and connecting key ideas and themes

Daily to-do list: A schedule showing the tasks, activities, and appointments due to occur during the day

Educated guessing: The practice of eliminating obviously false multiple-choice answers and selecting the most likely answer from the remaining choices

E-mail: Electronic mail, a system of communication that permits users to send and receive messages via the Internet

Essay questions: Test questions that require the creation of a fairly extended, on-the-spot composition, written in expository form

Evaluation: An assessment of the match between a product or activity and the goals it was intended to meet

Extemporaneous talk: An unprepared, off-the-cuff oral presentation

External attribution: The belief that events are caused by factors outside of oneself, over which one has little control

Fill-in questions: Test questions that require examinees to add one or more missing words to a sentence or series of sentences

Flash cards: Note cards that contain key pieces of information that are to be remembered

Freewriting: A technique involving continuous, nonstop writing, without self-criticism, for a fixed period of time

Frontmatter: The preface, introduction, and table of contents of a book

Hardware: The monitor, keyboard, mouse, and system unit (or CPU) of a computer

Hearing: The involuntary act of sensing sounds

Information management: The ability to find, harness, and use knowledge

Interlibrary loan: A system by which libraries share resources, making them available to patrons of different libraries

Internal attribution: The belief that events are caused by one's own behavior and effort

Internet: A vast network of interconnected computers that share information around the world

Life timeline: A long-term schedule of plans and intended accomplishments, covering the entire life span

Link: A means of "jumping" from one Web page to another automatically

Listening: The voluntary act of focusing on sounds and making sense of them

Listserv: A subscription service through which members can post and receive messages via e-mail on general topics of shared interest

Long-term goals: Aims relating to major accomplishments that take some time to achieve

Master calendar: A schedule showing the weeks of a longer time period, such as a college term, with all assignments and important activities noted on it

Matching questions: Sets of test questions that present two lists of related information, arranged in column form, which examinees must link

Memory consolidation: The process by which the physical links between brain cells that represent memory become fixed and stable over time

Meta-message: The underlying main ideas that a speaker seeks to convey through a spoken message

Method of loci: A memory technique by which the elements in a list are visualized as occupying the parts of a familiar place

Microform: A means of storing greatly reduced photographs of printed pages, which can be read using special microform readers; the two main types of microform are microfiche and microfilm

Mnemonics: Formal techniques used to make material more readily remembered

Motivation: The inner power and psychological energy that directs and fuels behavior

Multiple-choice questions: Test questions containing a question or statement followed by a number of response choices, from which the correct response must be selected

Newsgroup: An electronic Internet area in which users may post and read messages on topics of their own choosing

Overlearning: Studying and rehearsing material past the point of initial mastery, to the point at which recall becomes automatic

Peg method: A memory technique by which a series of memorized words is linked by images to a list of items to be remembered

Plagiarism: Taking credit for the words, thoughts, or ideas of another

Précis: A summary of a longer document

Priorities: The tasks and activities that one needs and wants to do, rank-ordered from most important to least important

Procrastination: The habit of putting off and delaying tasks that are to be accomplished

Reading style: A person's characteristic way of approaching reading tasks

Recall: A way to request library materials from another user who has them

Research notes: Notes taken, typically from written materials, for the purpose of writing a paper or preparing a report

Search engine: A computerized index to information on the World Wide Web

Short-answer questions: Test questions that require brief responses (at most a few sentences) in a kind of mini-essay

Short-term goals: Relatively limited steps toward the accomplishment of long-term goals

Software: Programs, or sets of instructions, that tell a computer what to do

Stacks: The shelves on which books and other materials are stored in a library

Study groups: Small, informal groups of students whose purpose is to help members work together and study for a test

Study notes: Notes taken, typically during a class lecture, for the purpose of reviewing material

Telnet: A dial-up communication system that permits users at remote locations to use computer databases and other resources housed on distant computers

Thesis: The main point of a paper, typically stating the writer's opinion about the topic of the paper

Time log: A record of how one spends one's time

True–false questions: Test questions that present statements about a topic that the examinee must identify as either accurate or inaccurate

Values: Beliefs that are held to be most important

Visualization: A memory technique by which images are formed to ensure that material arrives in long-term memory

Voice: The unique style of a writer, expressing the writer's outlook on life and past writing experiences

Web page: A location (or site) on the World Wide Web housing information from a single source, and (typically) links to other pages

Weekly timetable: A schedule showing all regular, prescheduled activities due to occur in the week, together with one-time events and commitments

World Wide Web: A highly graphical interface between users and the Internet that permits users to transmit and receive not only text, but pictorial, video, and audio information